Hand-Crafted Candy Bars

HAND-CRAFTED CANDY BARS

FROM-SCRATCH, ALL-NATURAL, GLORIOUSLY GROWN-UP CONFECTIONS

Susie Norris & Susan Heeger
Photographs by Joseph De Leo

CHRONICLE BOOKS
SAN FRANCISCO

ACKNOWLEDGMENTS

We would like to thank the following people, who, in different ways, helped guide and inspire us on the candy path, or walked it with us:

Jane and Jim, Frances, and Jim and Kelly Norris; Jason Epstein; Judy Miller; Helen Epstein and Peter Peter; Marcia, Mike, and Otto Heeger; Laura and Peter Bernhard; John Heeger and Hoang Nguyen; Andrea, Jim, Lily, Rosie, Lenard, and Elaine Steiner; David Draper; Audrey Augun; Gerson Zweifach; Tom Hentoff; Amy Treadwell; Joseph De Leo; Alice Chau; Carrie Purcell; Stuart Courtney; Natacha Leighton; Jackie Rogers; Carole Bloom; Peter Greweling; recipe-tester Christina Chung.

Very special thanks to our agents, Betsy Amster and Angela Rinaldi.

Library of Congress Cataloging-in-Publication Data available.

ISBN 978-1-4521-0965-7

Manufactured in China

FSC
www.fsc.org
MIX
Paper from responsible sources
FSC® C104723

Designed by Alice Chau and Lydia Ortiz
Illustrations by Lydia Ortiz

Food styling by Carrie Purcell
Prop styling by Paige Hicks

10 9 8 7 6 5 4 3 2 1

Chronicle Books LLC
680 Second Street
San Francisco, California 94107
www.chroniclebooks.com

This book is dedicated to:

Our families: Jacob, Sam, Natalie, and Thomas Epstein, and Rob and Simon Steiner, avid supporters of our candy-making adventures

Our dear friends: Jeremy and Dara Samuelson and Rebecca Farr, who helped us conceive and envision this project and without whom it wouldn't be

and to everyone who shares our candy-bar passion.

CHAPTER 4
DREAM BARS

Healthier, Spicier, Sexier

Candy *can* be good for you, especially if you make it yourself, using premium dark chocolate and loading in the walnuts, dried blueberries, and citrus zest, and lots of flavors-du-jour in the food world (green tea, black sesame, chipotle), which pair beautifully with chocolate. We'll give you recipes to prove our point, along with a Mix-and-Match Chart to help you craft your personal version of a dream bar.

CHAPTER 5
CANDY-BAR BASICS

Fundamental Recipes and Techniques

Going from candy-lover to candy-maker can be a pretty straightforward transformation if you've got the tools. It's also very satisfying, in the old-fashioned, deep-heart vein of hand-crafting in the kitchen.

CHAPTER 6
GILDING THE LILY

Dressing Bars for Dessert

While hand-crafted candy bars hardly need elaboration, they will show up even more fetchingly on a plate if you crown them with Dark-Chocolate Flowers or a soupçon of Caramel Sauce.

LOVING CANDY BARS

An Action Plan

CRAZY FOR CANDY

We're crazy about candy bars. We grew up with them, swapped them with our friends at school, ate them in movies, sneaked them home past our parents, who worried about our teeth. Even their wrappers delighted us. Cherished icons of our childhoods, these candy bars have stayed with us ever since. They've grown a little smaller and mutated into "fun sizes" for Halloween and dark and crunchy versions that expand our choices at the checkout. Still, they're what we know, what we remember. They're essentially the same.

What makes them great? Their combination of nostalgia and convenience: A candy bar is a small gift you can give yourself any time of day—an intense, concentrated pleasure to keep or share and repeat as often as you please. It's easy to find, cheap to buy, a little nothing with a big payoff.

COMRADES-IN-CANDY

Just how much that little nothing means hit home for us a few months ago. The two of us, who have a long, shared history with chocolate—and in particular, candy bars—had dinner with a bunch of friends. The talk turned to food and then to sweets, and suddenly, we were all shouting names of our favorites! The debate got so emotional that we realized we weren't alone. Everyone was obsessed! We all had our opinions, and in marketing terms, our dedicated buying habits. Dark chocolate, milk chocolate, almonds, no almonds. Some of us were big on crunch, others on smoothness; some favored many layers, others at most two.

CANDY CRITIQUE

But as we kept on talking, something else became clear: As passionate as we all were, and as hooked on our versions of the ideal bar—completely uniform and predictable every time—we realized we also occasionally wanted more. We faced the fact that as candy bars have stayed the same, we haven't. While our mothers thawed frozen peas and swore by *The Joy of Cooking*, we click on *Top Chef*, scan food blogs, follow chefs and restaurants, own knife sets, and make jam. Having read *Food Rules* by Michael Pollan, we're uncomfortable with food that's too processed. We like simple—but really good. And we're willing to spend time—and a little extra money—making it.

All this suddenly led us to the conclusion that candy bars could be different. Fresher, purer. For what they cost in fat and calories, they could be made with top chocolate, fresh nuts, and, please, no high-fructose corn syrup! But for this to happen, we would need to make them ourselves.

SIZING 'EM UP

Here are a few facts: Mass-produced candy bars require a long shelf life so they can make their way from factories to warehouses to stores to customers around the world. Manufacturers add preservatives to keep the dairy ingredients from spoiling. They also have to design the candy bars for portability, so they stack with tight efficiency into packing crates but don't arrive battered and squashed at the end of their trip. That's why the wrappers are full of zesty charm and the bars inside are no-frills bricks.

Nevertheless, we keep craving our candy bars, along with other sweets. The United States is one of the world's leading candy consumers, despite dicey economic times. Today, though consumers are carefully watching their budgets, they're willing to spend even more for high-end candy. This trend is linked to strong public interest in the health benefits of dark chocolate and a move toward premium and responsibly manufactured (organic, fair-trade) products. Another factor, of course, is superior taste.

MAKING GOOD GREAT

Should it really surprise us that a chocoholic used to the scant cocoa content of much commercial candy would find religion in the first bite of an artisan bar made with 72 percent cocoa? It happens every day. It happened to both of us. And it gave us an idea: While we're hardly going to give up the sweet, nostalgic candy bars we love, let's also make our own, inspired by the originals but more luxurious!

The result, *Hand-Crafted Candy Bars*, is a candy cookbook full of flavor-forward interpretations of what makes candy bars great. Among our recipes, you'll find chic, new confectionary creations that remind you of why you fell in love with candy bars in the first place.

From there, we'll hand you the tools to customize freely, to embellish your bars or reinvent them, to give free reign at last to the candy artist inside you.

We've all spent time making pies and cakes from scratch—and enjoyed the impact of these on people we cook for. Yet hand-crafted candy can be even more dramatic and intensely flavored, not to mention highly unexpected. Your dinner guests may think they know candy bars because they've eaten them forever. *You* will shatter this illusion with a kind of magic that leaves ordinary sweets in the dust.

This is a book we were born to write. One of us, Susie Norris, is a former television executive who chucked the business for a second career as a chocolatier and pastry chef/instructor and recently wrote the book *Chocolate Bliss*, a celebration of the origins, uses, and many pleasures of chocolate. The other, Susan Heeger, has also written widely about food (coauthor of *From Seed to Skillet*, a gardening guide and cookbook) and is just as wild about candy, which she never quite got enough of as a child but has made up for nicely as a grown-up.

OUR CANDY PLAN

Sitting together at that dinner table, it just clicked that the time was right for us to put together our shared candy-bar lust with the food knowledge we've acquired to take our beloved bars to another level.

Imagine this: With artisan candies you make at home, you can choose the freshest, best-tasting ingredients to craft bars as they should be—thick and richly layered with caramel or nougat, crunchy with toffee or nuts, generously coated with fine dark or milk chocolate. Delicious enough to satisfy any connoisseur's cravings, they're also so pretty to look at you *will* want to serve them for dessert—decorated, on a plate. Inspired by the classics, this book will teach you how to pair high-quality flavors with artistic flourishes to take candy bars from the ordinary to the sublime.

ARE THEY WORTH THE WORK?

Absolutely. And they may be less involved than you imagine. Far from the territory of experts, candy making is accessible to anyone with a sweet tooth and a wooden spoon. Whether you're a novice in the kitchen or a seasoned cook, all you need are a few basic tools, some chocolate and vanilla, lots of sugar, and a little imagination.

Most bars boil down to simple combinations of components. One popular bar, for instance, is vanilla shortbread, caramel, and milk chocolate; another is nougat, peanut caramel, and milk chocolate. With a few basic candy-making techniques—and top ingredients—this book shows you how to work with similar elements, adding here, subtracting there, to devise entirely new, hand-crafted bars. Picture one made with real cream and butter caramel (no preservatives or additives), sea-salted peanuts, deep dark chocolate from Venezuela, and even marzipan rosebuds. Or imagine a bar you can't find in any store—one formulated in your mind and tailored to your tastes, or your boyfriend's or sister's. This book teaches everything you need to make these visions come true, and then some.

But here comes our disclaimer: Our bars, though inspired by classic candy bars we love, are in no way copies of the originals, nor are they made, approved, or endorsed by any of the commercial candy companies. No one has paid us to tout their products, and, in fact, we won't mention them by name for trademark reasons. But as you read this book, you, too, will no doubt be calling up your personal candy-bar memories and enjoying thoughts of your favorites. It's only natural! They're part of the fabric of our history.

FUN FACTS, VITAL INFO

Throughout our book, sidebars will pop up, full of historical facts, additional how-to ideas, and trouble-shooting recipe tips. Why does chocolate boost your mood? We'll tell you. How do you make your own vanilla? We'll show you. What's the fix if your fondant's grainy instead of smooth? We'll guide you through the problem.

To many of us, candy bars are an anytime, anywhere symbol of pleasure, reward, affection. They feed our souls, fill our senses, make us happy. If you love candy bars the way we do, as the first, the last, the ultimate piece of heaven in your hand, this book is for you.

CHAPTER 1

BREAKING IT DOWN

Candy-Bar Elements, Ingredients, and Tools

What Is a Candy Bar—and What Should Be in It?

The first part of this question may seem silly, especially to those of us who eat them all the time. But consider the racks of sweets near the register in a supermarket, or behind the counter at a movie. Is a box of creamy, chocolate-coated mints a candy bar? How about a bag of candy-coated chocolate buttons? Frankly, we'd like to throw our arms out and scoop them all into the pages of this book, but we've got to draw the line somewhere. So for now, we're going to say that a candy bar is an all-in-one-piece proposition, often layered, and almost inevitably, in our hands, drenched in chocolate. (Later, in chapter 3, we'll sneak in some of the bits and pieces—inspired by some of the nonbar classics we've just described—under the heading, Bits & Bites We Love: A Few Delicious Extras, just because we can't help ourselves.)

As commercial candy bars have demonstrated for decades, many flavors and textures play well with chocolate—caramel, nougat, nuts, crispy rice, peanut butter, toffee. Our news is how amazing a bar tastes if you make it with fresh, roasted peanuts; fragrant, premium vanilla; and higher-quality chocolate. Each flavor seems to intensify the others. We're going to show you how and then give you a list of the tools you need to make it happen for yourself. It took the two of us years of candy eating to understand how our favorite bars worked their magic, and a lot of fun sessions in the kitchen to learn how to put the right pieces together to craft our own. In fact, we traveled rather different routes to get to this point.

SUSIE'S CANDY CONFESSIONS

I am lucky to have a tooth left in my head. I ate candy bars nonstop in the back of my family's station wagon on the competitive swim-team circuit in 1960s Kentucky. We're talking long, boring car rides to swim meets and long, boring rides home. What better way to pass the time than to raid the stash of candy bars my folks always packed to provide us with our athletic energy. Or, more likely, to keep us from arguing in the back of the car. All hail to the candy-bar basket! We had the classics, but we were also fascinated with the new and trendy—a kind of stick candy billed as astronaut food, along with jawbreakers, wax lips, and candy cigarettes.

My love of chocolate turned serious when I met great European chocolate in France, as a teenager on a summer bike trip. I discovered that every village had a patisserie full of giant éclairs with thick stripes of chocolate on the top. They were made with wildly fresh and tasty ingredients—"local" cream and "artisan" chocolate—before anybody had coined the terms. Later, I went to college, and got on the career track back in the States, but a piece of me stayed behind, my bike propped up against an iron chair on a patisserie patio with a river view, Orangina in one hand, éclair in the other. My sweetest memories are forever intertwined with pastry shops, chocolate, sugar, and heavy cream.

I was a television executive for many years, and in that world, nobody cared much about desserts. Business lunches ended hastily, just as I was eyeing the dessert menu and preparing to order an extra-foamy cappuccino. I indulged my longings for chocolate and pastries by studying cookbooks, baking obsessively, and finally taking a course in professional baking at a Los Angeles cooking school. This eventually led to a new career as a chocolatier (my chocolate business is Happy Chocolates, an online artisan boutique), pastry chef, and culinary school instructor. Along the way, I enlisted my friends as tasters for my chocolate creations. Susan, my dear friend, was a particularly avid taster, who not only cheered me on but whose chocolate passion and mania for candy bars equaled mine. It's not surprising, really, that the two of us were destined to team up.

SUSAN'S CANDY CONFESSIONS

Unlike Susie, I was a candy-deprived child. My mother had bad teeth—the result, my father believed, of too many sweets in *her* youth, which led to severe restrictions in our house. Unwelcome there, candy sneaked out, as forbidden things do, into other parts of my life, taking on a seductive thrill it has never lost for me. At the grocery store, I watched my mom unable to resist grabbing a few of her favorite bars, bolting them down guiltily in front of my brother, sister, and me, whom she'd promised my dad she wouldn't corrupt. When she finished shopping, she blushed as she pushed her sticky, chocolate-smudged wrappers at the cashier. Of course, there was also candy—heaps of it—lurking elsewhere in the world: Some of my friends had it at their houses. They brought it to school in their lunch boxes. Though I worried about getting caught, I tasted my first candy bar at a sleepover, my next at summer day camp.

Then there was Halloween, that amazing night dedicated to the glory of candy, when we Heegers were allowed only three pieces each. How liberating (yet admittedly shameful—shame on me!) it was to realize I could reject those excruciating choices. I could eat five or six and admit to only three!

Later, as I used my teenage freedom to go candy-bar crazy, I learned that my grandfather, my father's dad, had once owned a confectionary business—clearly a meaningful part of my DNA. It was a small, Los Angeles factory that "enrobed" candy bars, such a gorgeous word for the process of showering or drenching fillings with liquid chocolate! I sometimes hear it in my head as I savor my grown-up's right to eat candy whenever I please. For me, chocolate *is* the ultimate pleasure food, surpassing cake, pie, cookies, even ice cream, which I prefer (do I even need to say this?) with crushed candy bars in it.

Later I discovered European chocolate, and then certain premium American brands with much higher percentages of cocoa, the ground beans from cacao trees, the chocolate source. Superior chocolate—the exquisite balance of bitter-with-sweet, the melting smoothness of the real deal—snapped me awake to the realm of sensual, no-holds-barred confections and their almost limitless possibilities. Tasting small-batch, sea-salt caramels was a further awakening, and then Susie, in her white chef's coat, handed me a bar that she herself had made.

The Sweet Life: Then and Now

The handcrafted approach to candy is, like much in the food world now, more a return to something half-lost and forgotten than it is a true reinvention. In this delicious culinary moment we are rediscovering the deep, slow pleasures of the homemade that our grandmothers and great-grandmothers knew. Before the Industrial Revolution—and into its early days—common and special-occasion treats (bread, jam, pickles, desserts, candy) were made at home, in small batches. They varied according to region, season, family recipes. They were unique and imperfect, they demanded planning and time.

Eventually, once factories began turning them out in earnest, culinary staples were much more uniform and predictable, and easier to get. Mass-produced and "modern," they represented freedom, from all the time and work involved in making them, and progress, as measured by the wide range of newly available, convenient, machine-made commodities that never varied and came in crisp packages with sexy labels.

It's taken us years to realize that the trade-off—hand-crafted quality for ease—isn't the answer in every case.

There's a satisfaction in choosing your own ingredients and cooking something a little complicated. You don't have to wonder what's *in* it. Preservatives? Un-uh. Additives? *No.* And the act of making it can be relaxing, in contrast to the rest of your life (if it's as overloaded as ours), and just plain fun if you do it with a pal.

FROM CACAO TO CADBURY

Early homemade candy included sugared nuts, maple-syrup sweets, marzipan, caramels, and lemon drops. Chocolate wasn't eaten in the United States, or really anywhere, till the mid-1800s. Before that, here and in Europe, it was a drink made from cocoa mixed with sugar and either water or milk (though sometimes even beer or wine), generally for people royal or rich. Americans, in fact, showed up rather late to the chocolate party, considering that the tree from which cocoa comes, *Theobroma* (Greek for "food of the gods"), is native to our hemisphere. The first dedicated chocolate factory opened in Massachusetts in 1765 (see Chocolate and the Colonials, page 55), but as long ago as A.D. 250, the Olmec and the Maya drank a bitter concoction brewed from husked, fermented, roasted, and crushed cacao beans. The Aztec people developed a similar drink and used it in religious ceremonies. Spanish conquistador Hernando Cortés got his countrymen to take notice, and eventually, a sweet version of the Aztecs' spicier liquid chocolate seduced the citizens of Europe.

The French sipped chocolate enthusiastically (Marie Antoinette employed her own personal chocolate mix-master), and by the late 1600s, the English were drinking it hot, dissolved in milk, in public "chocolate houses" dedicated to its pleasures. When it arrived in the American colonies around the mid-1700s, it was still a thick and somewhat heavy brew, with a high percentage of cocoa butter that British connoisseurs had tried to cut with additives such as arrowroot and potato starch. But it was Dutch chemist Coenraad Van Houten who solved the problem in 1828 with a machine press that ground and heated cacao beans, producing liquid butter that was then poured off, leaving a paste called chocolate liquor. When the liquor hardened into powdery, cake-like cocoa solids, it was easy to dissolve in liquid for a lighter drink.

In 1847, English chocolatier Joseph Fry blended some of the butter back into the liquor, added sugar, and molded the mix into a rather coarse, eating bar. Others followed with their own versions—Englishman John Cadbury and Swiss duo Daniel Peter and Henri Nestlé, who swirled in condensed milk to create the aptly named milk chocolate in 1875. Soon, Rodolphe Lindt, a fellow Swiss invented a "conching" machine that mixed and kneaded chocolate to a melting smoothness. In the early 1900s, refrigeration supported the year-round manufacture and sale of chocolate—which otherwise melts between 86 and 90°F/32 and 34°C—and the proliferation of railroads helped spread the love to people eager to enjoy it.

HELLO, HERSHEY

Arguably, no one plunged into the chocolate world with quite the gusto of Milton Hershey, America's most famous confectioner, who'd already grown rich on caramels by the time he spotted German chocolate-crafting machines at Chicago's 1893 Columbian Exposition (also known as the Chicago World's Fair). He bought some for himself and by 1900 had democratized consumption of this formerly exclusive

sweet by cranking out nickel chocolate bars in his Pennsylvania factory, which became the heart of a whole chocolate-themed town.

Other companies followed. During World War I, several were hired by the U.S. Army to make chocolate in giant blocks for overseas troops. When these "doughboys" came home, they wanted more, and during the 1920s, many much-loved bars were invented. The number of distinct candy bars on sale in the United States rose at one point to 40,000, except that they weren't all nationally distributed. Hershey and Chicago-based Mars figured distribution out early and became two of the best-known brands of all time. Hershey's product, which Milton Hershey cannily sold not just in candy stores but also grocery stores, gas stations, and drugstores, and which carried the early label, "A Nourishing Food," became synonymous with the American chocolate bar itself.

CHOCOLATE, CHALLENGED

Of course, since the first nickel bar rolled off the line, changes have hit the candy business. Like everything else, the cost of ingredients (sugar, vanilla, cacao beans, and especially cocoa butter, highly valued in the cosmetics

trade) has risen, putting a strain on what's long been a low-cost product. To stay competitive, some companies have had to reduce the percentage of pricey items like cocoa butter in their bars, replacing them with other vegetable fats (including trans fats such as partially hydrogenated palm oil) as well as emulsifiers, stabilizers, synthetic flavors, colors, and other additives.

Then, too, certain disturbing truths have come to light about cacao farming's environmental and human costs in the tropical places where the trees thrive—Africa, Indonesia, and South America among them. These revelations have spawned calls for better forest preservation, organic pest controls, more sensitive harvesting techniques, and an end to the child and slave labor that for centuries have kept chocolate cheap and plentiful. Chocolate manufacturers have vowed to correct the problem, but progress reports are mixed. Awareness of chocolate's shady side—along with recent news about the health benefits of chocolate that's darker and more pure—have moved many of us to change our thinking about chocolate, and to search out brands that use organically grown and responsibly harvested beans and add little to them besides sugar and vanilla.

The Artisan Option

But there's another way, too, to bypass some of the candy industry's sticky issues. We make pies, don't we? We make cakes. Many of us know our way around a kitchen. If we craft our own candy bars, we can start with organically produced chocolate, loaded with heart-healthful cacao, and grown under Fair Trade regulations that ensure farmers just prices while strengthening their communities with amenities like schools and clean drinking water. We can ax the palm oil and the chemical additives, use good butter, fresh nuts, and pure vanilla—an element that, all on its own, as you'll see on the following pages, kicks the enterprise up a notch. In the same way, organic peanut butter may offer stronger, more nuanced flavor than a nonorganic and highly processed alternative, or a coarse salt may provide more texture than a fine one. Each item on your ingredient list affects the outcome of your candy bar in large or small ways—all worth considering as you swing down this road with us.

CHOOSING CHOCOLATE

There are so many great chocolates to work with, from Valrhona, Barry Callebaut, Amedei, and other

Cacao vs. Cocoa

Language in the chocolate production process borrows from native Aztec (or Nahuatl), Latin, Spanish, and English. The word cacao (pronounced ka-KOW) originates from the Aztec. When we refer to the tree, its pods, its seeds (or beans, as they are commonly called because they look like beans), we use the word cacao. When we refer to the seeds as they are processed for chocolate production, we begin to use the word cocoa. So, as seeds are taken from their pods and fermented, then dried, then hulled for chocolate production, we call them cocoa beans. The broken pieces, cocoa nibs, are the raw material from which cocoa mass or cocoa liquor is made. If all the cocoa butter is removed from the mass, it is called cocoa powder or cocoa for short. Just to confuse matters further, premium chocolate labels sometimes read "78 percent cacao" or "82 percent cacao." This refers to the percentage of cocoa mass (pure, unsweetened, crushed cocoa beans) in the chocolate bar as opposed to other ingredients like sugar or milk powder.

European companies, as well as fine United States offerings, including Scharffen Berger and E. Guittard. Some successful artisan brands (Scharffen Berger, Dagoba, and Green & Black's) have recently been acquired by larger chocolate corporations, but they remain high-quality choices. These companies produce excellent versions of couverture, i.e., professional-grade chocolate made with high cocoa content, cocoa butter, and only minimal additives and all are easy to find, either online or in

stores. Using one of the top brands or the equivalent (a premium Fair Trade brand like Dagoba, Endangered Species, or Green & Black's Organic) will give your bars a better texture and aroma, and a richer taste than you'd get with the piled-in sugar and fake flavorings of cheap chocolate. Naturally, you're going to pay more, but the rewards, we promise, will be big.

Chocolate falls into four main categories: cocoa powder, dark, milk, and white. Cocoa powder and the darkest chocolates have the strongest taste, the most nutrients, and the most purity. Unsweetened cocoa powder is a key component in cakes and brownies, but it isn't especially useful in candy bars (except as decoration or an ingredient in our cookies), so we won't say much about it here. Dark chocolate runs from unsweetened to semisweet and bittersweet, with a cocoa volume of 60 percent or more. The higher that number is, the healthier the chocolate. Very dark chocolate provides more of the chemicals that send blood efficiently to your heart and can potentially (if you don't go chocolate-mad) help stave off cancer, heart disease, and the effects of aging. Less good-for-you milk chocolate is just dark chocolate that's further processed with extra sugar and milk powder, its cocoa content ranging from 38 to 50 percent. The fourth, white chocolate, is not, strictly speaking, chocolate but a sweet mixture of cocoa butter, milk powder, sugar, and flavorings.

Historically, candy bars, particularly those for American markets, have relied heavily on milk chocolate, and so do many in this book, though we suggest using quality brands of milks, and those with higher cocoa content. But imagine a dark-dipped take on a caramel-and-nougat log or peanut-butter cup.

As we've said before, once you learn the ropes, you can change the rules, or the recipes, as you see fit. You might decide you like the dark version better than the more traditional milk.

In general, the chocolate you choose will depend on your goals for a particular bar. Which flavors do you want to emphasize and play off against others? Some milk chocolates have strong caramel notes that create an added, exquisite layer of flavor for a candy bar with lots of caramel inside. On the other hand, a dark chocolate with very assertive fruit notes provides a tangy contrast to a buttery caramel center.

As you experiment with chocolate, in all its personalities and shadings, your tastes will evolve. And you'll find that when you make changes in your chocolate, the other elements change too: the amounts and kinds of sugars and vanillas; your pick of nuts; your choice of salts. So we need to think about these, too.

THE SKINNY ON SUGAR AND OTHER SWEETENERS

Sugar gets a lot of bad press, and often, deservedly so. It's no news that if you eat enough sugar, your teeth will rot, your clothes won't fit, and you might develop heart disease or diabetes. The real villain, though, is not your beautiful, hand-crafted, special-occasion candy bar. As Vermont pastry chef Gesine Bullock-Prado, author of the book *Sugar Baby*, pointed out in the online magazine Zester Daily, the real villain is the hidden depth charge in processed food (see Candy Sugar vs. Hidden Sugar, page 87). It's the high-fructose corn syrup lurking in commercial salad dressings and frozen chicken dinners. It's the daily, unexamined soft-drink habit, responsible for a third of the sugar Americans consume. If you look sharp for those

High on Chocolate?

In the midst of a bad day, popping a square or two of chocolate seems to make things better. While some say it's because chocolate contains certain stimulating "happy" chemicals (including tryptophan, anandamide, caffeine, and phenylethylamine), these aren't present in large enough quantities to do the job. More likely explanations for the pick-me-up are chocolate's sugar and cocoa-butter content, and its smell, taste, and feel in your mouth. Your happy memories of eating it in the past also add to the pleasure boost.

sneaky stowaways, and eat plenty of good, pure, whole meals à la Michael Pollan's directive ("Eat food, not too much, mostly plants"), you can save your sweet tooth for a consciously enjoyed, unapologetic, sugar-packed treat.

And now that we have *that* behind us, let's consider those fabulous crystals, powders, and syrups that make our candy *sweet*! White granulated table sugar is the type we use most in candy making. A disaccharide, it's a compound mix of two simple sugars, fructose and glucose (also sometimes called dextrose). Many of our recipes call for table sugar with a lesser amount of corn syrup—a liquid suspension of mostly glucose, derived from corn. The corn syrup kicker may be there to prevent candy from crystallizing, or to change its consistency—make it thick and chewy, for example. But corn syrup is not to be confused with the high-fructose corn syrup (HFCS) we referred to previously. HFCS is a corn syrup that's chemically treated to boost the content of the fructose, which is the sweeter of the two simple sugars. Thanks to government corn subsidies, it's cheap to make, and finds its way, perceptibly and otherwise, into much of our packaged food. In a Princeton University study, rats fed a diet that included HFCS gained significantly

more weight than those on a calorically equivalent diet that traded table sugar for HFCS. The HFCS group also showed unusually high increases in body fat and triglycerides, a risk factor for heart disease.

Clearly, we're going to steer away from *that*. But what of the other forms sugar takes—premium options that include such tantalizers as Belgian pearl sugar, traditionally used in waffle-making; amber sugar recommended for "high tea service"; and a certain brand of beautiful brown sugar cubes produced in the Congo and packaged in France? We have to admit, that last product comes in a very seductive box, and we have occasionally bought it just for that!

But the fact is, white table sugar from the grocery store, along with a bottle of corn syrup and an occasional addition of brown sugar (which, given its higher molasses content, can contribute a nutty flavor), are all you need to make most of our artisan candy bars. Whenever our recipes call for sugar, we're referring to everyday, granulated sugar that you can buy in the grocery store. Superfine versions (which also come in the form of castor sugar or "baker's special fine") dissolve faster, but are more appropriate for applications like meringues. Coarse sugar, sometimes

called sanding or crystal sugar, is a decorator's tool (think of Christmas sugar cookies), and confectioners', or powdered sugar, makes a good dusting for a plated sweet or a white glaze for a cake. We use these in a few of our recipes, but we will always be specific if the sugar we're calling for is anything other than grocery store granulated, the most common of table sugars. For the most part, we save our pennies for this next ingredient . . .

THE POTENT PERFUME OF VANILLA

For centuries, chocolate and vanilla have been a sexy power couple, natural flavor partners that each spark something wonderful in the other. Vanilla was introduced to Europe by none other than Cortés, the Spanish explorer who first sipped both together in the frothy chocolate drink mixed for him by the Aztecs. Some of the finest vanilla still hails from Mexico, the native home of the rare orchid that produces vanilla beans. Papantla in Veracruz, a center of this orchid's cultivation, is called "the city that perfumes the world." This gives you some idea of vanilla's potency, and the fact that, interestingly, its value lies more in its aroma and its ability to heighten other flavors than in its taste.

Homemade Vanilla Extract

The closer you get to vanilla, the more you understand the potency of the tiny seeds packed into their slender pods. Vanilla extract, the fragrant infusion of vanilla seeds in alcohol, is easy to make using beans you buy online or in specialty cooking stores. To add extra flavor notes, you can experiment with various liqueurs, swapping in Grand Marnier or brandy for the rum and vodka. Since alcohol is a preservative, the resulting extract will keep indefinitely. This also gives you a great way to recycle vanilla pods after you have used their seeds to flavor candy bars.

4 vanilla beans

1 cup/240 ml dark rum

1/2 cup/120 ml vodka

Lay the vanilla beans on a cutting board, split them open lengthwise, scrape out the seeds using the back of a paring knife, and reserve the pods. In a 1-pt/480-ml lidded glass jar, combine the rum and vodka, mix in the vanilla seeds, add the pods, and cover. Shake well, and then again every few days. After a week, the extract is ready to use, but its flavor deepens the longer it sits. It keeps indefinitely, especially if you refresh it with alcohol when it runs low and regularly add in gently used pods when you have them.

The second-most expensive spice after saffron, vanilla requires much time and labor to get from bloom to bottle. Its climbing vines, in the rain forests of Guadeloupe, Indonesia, Madagascar, Mexico, Reunion, and Papua New Guinea, sprout fleeting blossoms, which, once pollinated (by hand), take nine months to mature into long seed pods ready to harvest, dry, cure, and sell in bundles graded for quality. The vanilla extract we use in cooking is made from crushed vanilla pods suffused in alcohol. Synthetic, or imitation vanilla—called vanillin, which, confusingly, is also the name of the chemical compound that gives real vanilla most of its flavor—is made from clove trees, waste paper pulp, or coal tar. Not surprisingly, given that the real thing contains many more elements, and thus flavor notes, than just vanillin, its complex taste and aroma can't easily be cooked up in a lab.

So, for starters, as you equip your candy-bar kitchen, it's important to spring for the pure, not the fake. Next, you must decide whether your candy craft is worth splurging on a premium vanilla—from a top U.S. company like Nielsen & Massey, Madécasse, the Vanilla Co., or the Hawaiian Vanilla Co., or one of the best imports, such as German-Canadian Aust & Hachmann. Will your candy bar taste richer with one of these instead of a supermarket brand? We would say yes. The harder question involves choosing the best vanilla from among many good ones you'll find in stores and online. Since that's partly a subjective challenge, the answer is: Try several.

While commercial vanilla extract comes mainly from two varieties of beans, planifolia and tahitensis, each vanilla growing region has a distinctive *terroir*, the vinophile's term for a crop's flavor-distinguishing essence of place and soil. Madagascar, Indonesia, and Mexico produce planifolia vanilla (also called Madagascar, Bourbon, or true vanilla) with an especially distinct bouquet and unique flavor characteristics. But growers in the South Pacific, especially Papua New Guinea, cultivate tahitensis, known for its fruity, floral extract, which is preferred by some pastry chefs. As with chocolate, your own taste preferences will become clearer as you experiment. And of course, price will play a role too. Some premium brands may cost twice as much as their competitors.

NUTS THAT MAKE A DIFFERENCE . . . AND NUTS THAT DON'T

Here's our chance to plug one of our favorite superstores, Costco. Not only is it an ethical company that treats its employees well and gives back to the communities where it does business, but it's a great place to buy nuts! You can go to a gourmet-food boutique and pay a lot for a tiny bag or you can hit your nearest Costco for a big haul at a small price. You don't just get heaps of pecans there either; you get pecans that are salted correctly for use in baking (just enough, not too much) and lightly roasted, so they don't dry out when you do bake them. Nor do you need worry about using up those bulk buys before the nuts go stale: Stashed in your freezer in a zip-top plastic bag, they'll keep almost indefinitely.

Our main exceptions to these Costco runs are when we buy Marcona almonds (sweet, plump Spanish imports), for

decoration, or when a recipe calls for "blister peanuts," which are boiled or soaked to remove their skins and then fried or roasted unto blistering for extra crunch. (Both are available at Trader Joe's or online.)

If you prefer your nuts raw and unprocessed, roast them yourself before mixing them into a bar unless they're going into the cookie component. There, they'll roast on their own as the cookie bakes.

NAVIGATING SALT

Salt sparks sweet flavors, giving them depth and interest that the merely sugary doesn't have on its own. Without a bit of salt, sweet gets cloying. The contrast is important. Add too much, though, and salt overpowers other tastes. As with so much in this world, the balance is crucial. But the balance depends on what else is in the mix.

One sweet-salt pair that's recently been on our candy-loving radar occurs in artisan salt caramels, a popular treat right now. Caramel itself, as we'll discuss in the next chapter, is a bit of a paradox in that it's sugar-based, yet adds a subtle bitterness to sweets. If you make it with coarse salt, the larger grains of which don't dissolve as well or as evenly as fine, the salt stands out

perceptibly amid the melted sugar, enhancing both, so your sweet caramel has a salty side. You'll get even more impact if you mix in the salt once the caramel has cooled, or you sprinkle it on the finished caramels, as many professional confectioners do.

Salt for cooking comes in three forms. Fine-textured table salt is usually iodine-enriched and has been in the United States since the 1920s, to reduce the incidence of thyroid conditions caused by mineral deficiencies. Kosher salt, generally coarser grained, is free of additives and also available in a finer flake. Sea salt, which hails from around the globe (and is sold in named varieties reflecting origin), is distinguished by different textures and colors, ranging from pearl-white to pink and even black. It may contain minerals and even smell faintly of the ocean. La Baleine, from France, is fine-grained and dissolves more uniformly than Maldon, an English sea salt with large, crunchy flakes. Fleur de sel, hand-harvested and thus often more expensive than other sea salts, may have a higher mineral content.

Very much a trend in the artisan-chocolate world, colored sea salts have a role to play when we dress candy bars for guests: Picture our hand-crafted Over the Moon (page 30), dusted with Himalayan pink sea salt, presented on a pink Fiestaware plate!

Unless we specify an alternative, you can use either fine kosher or fine sea salt in our recipes, since what we're after is a well-dissolved and evenly distributed salt taste to balance the sweet. With cooked ingredients such as caramel and fondant, we add salt late in the recipe, while our mixture is still hot, so the crystals melt and blend well with the other flavors.

BETTER BUTTER

Without butter, we candy-bar makers would be lost, especially when it comes to bars layered with caramel or toffee. Butter gives both a certain richness on the tongue, a note of luxury that deepens the satisfaction of eating them. So one of the first questions that arises is whether to use unsalted or salted butter. Each one has its devotees. Many pastry chefs prefer unsalted, because the amount of salt in salted butter varies widely, from as little as 1/4 tsp to as much as 3/4 tsp in 1/2 cup/115 g. Adding your own salt separately gives you more control over the saltiness of the end product. On the other hand, salt acts as a preservative in butter, so salted butter stays fresh longer—which

isn't a problem if you refrigerate your unsalted butter. But one more plus with the salted option is that it can be a stabilizer during the cooking process for both toffee and caramel, preventing the separation of butter and sugar once you've poured your mix on a baking sheet. If you use unsalted butter, add 1/4 tsp of salt for every 1/2 cup/115 g, unless the recipe already calls for it.

Does the quality of commercial butters vary enough that you need to splurge and buy the best? In many candy cases, it's a good idea. Premium butter, which may be labeled European-style, or may actually come from France, Ireland, or some other place across the pond, contains less water and a higher butterfat content, which translates into a richer taste. Since you're using butter *for* that richness, aiming higher makes sense. But the options can be dizzying. Plugra, a U.S. product that's labeled European-style, is a darling among chefs, but it can cost more than twice the price of Land O'Lakes, another American brand that gets high marks from tasters. (And Land O'Lakes also makes its own premium, "Ultra-Creamy" butter.) The Vermont Butter & Cheese Creamery is known for quality small-batch butter; Kerrygold Irish Butter comes from grass-fed, free-roaming Irish cows,

which, according to the company's website, boosts its beta-carotene content, giving it a more intense gold color. And let's not forget Lurpak Slightly Salted Butter from Denmark or the highly-touted French product, Président. Whichever you choose might depend on how flush you're feeling, or how much candy you plan to make. If you're crafting gift bars for someone special, grab the good stuff. You might want to experiment with several brands, which is what we like to do. But if you're not feeling flush at all, buy the Land O'Lakes. *Cook's Illustrated*, in a butter taste-off, listed it as "recommended," right along with the fancier brands.

Candy-Bar Toolbox

You may have most of these already in your kitchen. They're the basics, but they'll get you started, and you can add to them as you go.

» 1 heavy-bottomed saucepan or soup pot with a capacity of 2 to 3 qt/2 to 2.8 L (A Le Creuset casserole is perfect.)
» 1 small saucepan, 1½ qt/1.4 L
» 2 medium saucepans, approximately 3.5 qt/3.3 L
» 1 colander
» 1 or more long-handled wooden spoons
» 2 large nonstick spatulas
» 1 long, narrow offset spatula (optional)
» 1 digital or candy thermometer
» 3 sturdy, rimmed cookie sheets (see Note)
» One 9-by-12-in/23-by-30.5-cm baking rack
» 2 small metal bowls
» 2 medium metal bowls
» 1 large metal bowl
» 1 large (about 9-by-14-in/23-by-35.5-cm) ovenproof glass or ceramic baking dish
» Two 8-in/20-cm square baking pans or 8-in/20-cm round cake pans
» One 12-cup muffin pan
» An electric mixer with paddle and whisk attachments
» A sifter (for powdered sugar, cocoa powder, and flour)
» 1 box zip-top plastic bags, gallon size
» 1 medium ladle (optional)
» 1 biscuit cutter (approximately 2-in/5-cm diameter)
» 2 piping bags, canvas or disposable plastic (optional)
» Bamboo skewers (optional)
» A marble slab, 18 by 18 in/46 by 46 cm (optional but highly useful and recommended; see Shopping Resources Guide, page 150)

» 2 or 3 chocolate molds (optional)
» 2 chocolate dipping forks (optional)
» 2 madeleine pans or seashell cookie sheets (optional; see Shopping Resources Guide, page 150)
» 1 rotary fan for cooling chocolate (optional)
» 2 squeeze bottles (optional)

Note: Rimmed cookie sheets are known to professional cooks as half-sheets or sheet pans; in our recipes, we refer to these simply as baking sheets.

Gift for You? Weighing a Marble Slab

You see them in old-fashioned fudge kitchens, and cookbooks tout them because they cool fondant quickly and keep pie dough cold while you work. But with all the gadgets in your cupboards, must you rush out and buy a marble slab? Not really. However, we use them ourselves. Marble slabs are great for hot sugar syrups poured from a pot, such as fondant and fudge. Their smoothness and natural coldness allow the syrups to cool quickly and evenly, so their crystals form in the small, uniform shapes that create the melting texture of good fudge. True, you can cool your syrup in a chilled pan, as we've instructed in our fudge recipes, but as your candy-making skills—and enthusiasm—grow, you might decide you need a slab. This, along with chocolate dipping forks, a chocolate chipper, and a couple of new nonstick spatulas (in candy colors, of course), could go on your gift list for anyone who appreciates what you've been cooking.

CHAPTER 2
BORN-AGAIN BARS

A Fresh Take on a Candy Classic

Say goodbye to any reservations you have about your candy-making skills. Crafting candy is not just fun, it's pretty straightforward. Whether you're a new or experienced cook, you'll be able to follow our step-by-step instructions for how to create and assemble the layers of each bar—from boiling the caramel to tempering chocolate for the finishing dip.

In this chapter and the next three, you'll find the recipes you need to craft and assemble candy bars, some inspired by familiar classics, some based on super-healthful alternatives, some even your own inventions. Since each bar generally consists of a few components, we list these in the recipe. The instructions for making each component—what we call our Fundamental Recipes and Techniques—can all be found in Chapter 5: Candy Bar Basics. So you'll read through your master recipe, make the basics from the referenced pages in chapter 5, and return to the master for assembly. That's it.

Some candy-crafting techniques may seem unfamiliar at first, in the same way that handling pie dough is to someone who's never done it. But as you work with the ingredients, you'll begin to develop a feel for what you're doing, just as you do with pie. Our goal is to sweep away the mystery surrounding candy until it becomes as unintimidating to you as other desserts, and more satisfying if you love it as we do. As you learn and gain confidence, you can get more inventive, drawing on elements from the convenient Mix-and-Match Chart that we provide on page 99.

Even before you reach that point, we predict you'll be feeling a certain meditative calm that comes with doing many kinds of old-fashioned handwork purely for the fun of it. No one's paying you or grading you; you're focusing on the small, incremental details of a job done right, all for the pleasure of handing a homemade bar to a friend or dinner guest. What could be sweeter?

CHOCOLATE & NUTS INSIDE & OUT

Many fine candy bars spring from the basic combination of fondant, nuts, and chocolate. Some offer the combo with no chocolate; others roll the fondant in peanuts, then give it a chocolate dip. Our interpretation takes a similar approach but wraps the fondant around roasted almonds before the peanut roll and chocolate plunge. Voilà, nuts inside and out.

MAKES
about
30
BARS

TIME NEEDED
about
1 HR **30** MIN

1 Line a baking sheet with parchment paper. Place the peanuts on a large plate.

2 After adding the vanilla to the fondant as directed, shape the fondant into small logs about 3 in/7.5 cm long and ½ in/12 mm thick. Press 3 whole almonds into the center of each log. Pinch the fondant around the almonds to encase them. Roll each log in the peanuts so they adhere to the fondant. Press the nuts in firmly, then set the bars on the prepared baking sheet.

3 Have the tempered chocolate at 90°F/34°C. Dip each log into the chocolate, remove it quickly with two forks or chocolate dipping forks, shake off the excess chocolate, and put on the baking sheet. Allow the chocolate to harden at room temperature for 20 minutes (a rotary fan aimed toward the logs speeds this up) or in the refrigerator for about 10 minutes. Serve at room temperature.

Store in an airtight container or a zip-top plastic bag at room temperature for 3 days, in the refrigerator for 2 weeks, or in the freezer for 2 months.

Variation: Nuts Inside & Out Make the nut-filled, nut-coated fondant bar, as directed, but hold the chocolate.

2 cups/230 g peanuts, roasted (see page 69)

1 batch **Fondant** (page 106)

2 cups/230 g whole almonds, roasted (see page 69)

1 batch **Tempered Milk Chocolate** (page 128)

over the moon

MAKES
about

30
BARS

TIME NEEDED
about

1ʜʀ **40**ᴍɪɴ

1 batch **Milk-Chocolate Caramel** (page 113)

1 batch **Soft Chocolate Nougat** (page 101)

2 tbsp barley malt syrup (see Shopping Resources Guide, page 150)

1 batch **Tempered Milk Chocolate** (page 128)

One well-known commercial candy bar was born after a father and son shared a malted milkshake and decided to re-create the experience in a confection. Inspired by the original, we crafted our own bar with rich, milk-chocolate caramel topped by fluffy chocolate nougat infused with barley malt syrup, dipped, of course, in more premium milk chocolate. To make a dark chocolate version, our Dark Side of the Moon, coat the bars in Tempered Dark Chocolate (page 126).

1 Line both a baking sheet and an 8-in/20-cm square or round baking pan with parchment paper or aluminum foil. Put a baking rack over the baking sheet.

2 Pour the caramel into the baking pan so that it is at least ½ in/12 mm thick. Allow it to cool for about 10 minutes, then refrigerate (see Note).

3 While preparing the nougat, after adding the vanilla and salt, stir in the malt syrup. Let cool for at least 10 minutes.

4 Remove the caramel from the refrigerator and cut into 3-in/7.5-cm logs.

5 Have the tempered chocolate at 90°F/34°C. Using a pastry brush or small paintbrush, paint the top of each log with the chocolate. Place the logs on the baking rack with the painted chocolate sides up. Refrigerate until chocolate sets, about 10 minutes. Once the chocolate on the bars has set, flip them over on the rack with the chocolate side facing down. Using a large table-spoon or piping bag, spread a layer of the nougat (at least ½ in/12 mm thick)

CONTINUED

over each bar, then pour more chocolate over the nougat, allowing the excess to drip through the rack onto the parchment. Refrigerate the finished bars for about 10 minutes to allow the chocolate to set. Serve at room temperature.

Store in an airtight container, a zip-top plastic bag, or plastic wrap at room temperature for 2 days, in the refrigerator for 1 week, or in the freezer for 1 month.

Note: A long chilling makes for caramel with a thicker texture, so this step can be done in advance and the caramel left to cool in the refrigerator overnight.

Too Precious to Toss: Recycled Chocolate

Often, when you temper chocolate—or just melt it for candy-bar coatings—you wind up with more than you need. What self-respecting chocolate lover would ever trash such treasure? Yet, aside from just devouring it straight from the bowl, how do you save it and use it later? The extra tempered chocolate can work for you in many ways: You can remelt it, make ganache with it, mix it into a warm caramel sauce, or even temper it again. Just pour the excess onto a baking sheet lined with parchment paper. Once it hardens, break it up and store it in a zip-top bag in a cool, dark spot or wrap it tightly in plastic wrap or aluminum foil until you're ready to use it.

CRISPY COOKIE CRUNCH

MAKES
about
30
PIECES

TIME NEEDED
about
1 HR 45 MIN

1 batch **Brown Sugar–Crisps**
(page 124), cooled

1 batch **Milk-Chocolate Ganache**
(page 119)

1 batch **Tempered Milk Chocolate**
(page 128)

The secret to this bar is the balance between snappy cookie and creamy candy. It has three overlapping components: cookie, cream, and chocolate. It's a fun recipe for two friends to make together. While one of you whips up the cookies and pops them in the oven, the other can make the Milk-Chocolate Ganache. Once the cookies bake and then cool, you can flip a coin as to who spreads them with the ganache and who tempers the milk chocolate for the coating.

1 Line two baking sheets with parchment paper.

2 With a rubber spatula or large spoon, spread each cooled crisp evenly with the ganache, then top with a second wafer to make a sandwich.

3 Have the tempered chocolate at 90°F/34°C. Dip each cookie sandwich into the chocolate and fish it out with two dinner forks or chocolate dipping forks. Shake off the excess chocolate, then slide the bars onto the prepared baking sheets. Allow them to set at room temperature (a rotary fan aimed toward the bars speeds this up) for 20 minutes, or in the refrigerator for 10 minutes. Serve at room temperature.

Store in an airtight container, a zip-top plastic bag, or plastic wrap at room temperature for 3 days, in the refrigerator for 2 weeks, or in the freezer for 2 months.

COCOA-NIB CARAMEL COOKIE STICKS

The crunchy cookie in each bite of these bars comes from a vanilla-rich version of *pâte sucrée*, a sweet French pastry dough. These artisan bars incorporate chewy caramel and milk chocolate for a harmonious mix of tastes and textures, accented by the toasty crunch of cocoa nibs.

MAKES
about

36
BARS

TIME NEEDED
about

1 HR 30 MIN

1 batch **Very-Vanilla Sugar Cookies** dough (page 123)

1 batch **Tempered Milk Chocolate** (page 128)

1 batch **Basic-Batch Caramel** (page 109)

1/2 cup/40 g cocoa nibs

1   Line a baking sheet with parchment paper or aluminum foil and place a baking rack over it. Line a second baking sheet with plastic wrap.

2   Form the cookie dough into 3-in/7.5-cm logs, each about ¾ in/2 cm thick. With the tip of a spoon, scrape out a deep trench on top of each log (this will be filled with caramel after the cookie is baked). Bake for about 20 minutes, until the logs are light golden brown around the edges.

3   Have the tempered chocolate at 90°F/34°C. With a small pastry brush or paintbrush, paint a thin layer of chocolate on the bottom of each cookie. Allow the cookies to set with the bottoms facing up. (If your kitchen is hot, a rotary fan aimed toward the cookies will speed the process, or refrigerate the cookies for about 10 minutes.)

4   After the caramel has cooled for about 20 minutes, stir in the cocoa nibs.

5   Once the chocolate has set, flip the cookies over and place on the baking rack. With a metal soup spoon, drizzle the cooled caramel into the trenches in the cookies and let set for about 10 minutes.

6   Move the caramel-covered cookies on their rack to the baking sheet lined with plastic wrap. Ladle a thick coating of chocolate over each cookie, and shake the baking rack to allow the excess chocolate to drip off onto the plastic wrap. Let the coated bars set at room temperature (again, a rotary fan aimed toward the bars will expedite the job) for about 20 minutes or in the refrigerator for about 10 minutes. Serve at room temperature.

Store in an airtight container or a zip-top plastic bag at room temperature for 3 days, in the refrigerator for 2 weeks, or in the freezer for 2 months.

What Are Cocoa Nibs?

Fermented, hulled, roasted, cracked cocoa beans, known as nibs, offer a pure and very healthful chocolate experience, since they have not been sweetened or mixed with any other additives. You can find them in grocery and health food stores and online. They're nutty tasting, lightly crunchy, and very chocolaty, with an interesting bitterness.

WHITE-CHOCOLATE COOKIES & CRUNCH BARS

MAKES
about

24 TO 30
PIECES

TIME NEEDED
about

1 HR 30 MIN

1 batch **Chocolate Sugar Cookies** (page 121)

1 batch **Hard Caramel** (page 114)

1 cup/115 g whole almonds, roasted (see page 69) and roughly chopped

1 batch **Tempered White Chocolate** (page 129)

White chocolate's inherent softness stems from the fact that it's simply cocoa butter, sugar, and milk powder—no cocoa solids—which also accounts for its creamy color. Here, we contrast this pleasing hue with pieces of dark chocolate cookie plus caramelized nuts for crunch.

1 Line a baking sheet or 8-in/20-cm round pan with parchment paper and set it aside.

2 Allow the cookies and caramel to cool, then crush them into very small pieces—about the size of chopped peanuts—and mix them with the almonds.

3 Have the tempered chocolate at 90°F/34°C. Add the cookie, caramel, and nut pieces to the chocolate. Mix lightly, then pour onto the prepared baking sheet. Allow to set in the refrigerator for 30 minutes. Break into pieces or cut into wedges and serve.

Store in an airtight container or a zip-top plastic bag at room temperature for 3 days or in the freezer for 2 months. (It's best not to store this one in the refrigerator, because the cookie pieces get soggy.)

DARK CHOCOLATE-DIPPED ALMOND COCONUT BARS

Our almond coconut bar makes the most of a sweet, nut-topped, coconut-cream center by covering it in very dark premium chocolate—a tempting contrast of sugary and sharp.

MAKES
about

16
BARS

TIME NEEDED
about

1HR

1 cup/115 g whole almonds

¾ cup/70 g powdered sugar, sifted

2 tbsp heavy cream

2 cups/190 g sweetened, shredded coconut

½ tsp salt

1 batch **Tempered Dark Chocolate** (page 126)

2 tbsp unsweetened cocoa powder (for decoration)

1   Preheat the oven to 350°F/180°C/gas 4. Prepare two baking sheets by lining them with parchment paper or aluminum foil.

2   Place the almonds on one baking sheet and bake for 10 to 15 minutes, until they are aromatic and lightly brown.

3   In a medium bowl, combine the sifted powdered sugar and cream with a rubber spatula or wooden spoon until you have a paste. Stir in the coconut and salt. Shape into 2-in/5-cm firmly packed logs, each with a slightly flattened top, and put the logs on the second baking sheet. Put 2 almonds on top of each log and push them gently but firmly into the coconut mixture. Refrigerate for about 20 minutes.

4   Remove the logs from the refrigerator. Have the tempered chocolate at 90°F/34°C. Dip each log into the chocolate. Use two dinner forks or chocolate dipping forks to fish the log out. Shake the logs carefully with the forks until excess chocolate drips off, then slide them onto the baking sheet originally used to toast the nuts, after brushing it off or relining with parchment paper. Using a sifter or tea strainer, dust each bar with a little cocoa powder while the chocolate is still moist. Let the chocolate set at room temperature (a rotary fan aimed toward the bars speeds this up) or refrigerate for about 10 minutes. Once the chocolate sets, serve the bars at room temperature.

Store in an airtight container, a zip-top plastic bag, or plastic wrap at room temperature for up to 3 days, in the refrigerator for 2 weeks, or in the freezer for 2 months.

CONTINUED

Variation: Milk Chocolate–Dipped Almond Coconut Bar For an even sweeter, creamier version, dip your bars in Tempered Milk Chocolate (page 128) instead of dark. The decorative dusting of cocoa powder will create a lovely color contrast.

Variation: Coconut Clouds Omit the nuts and proceed with the dark-chocolate dip and cocoa dusting for a simple, airy confection of coconut and chocolate.

Heavy Cream vs. Whipping Cream

Cream, the top layer of milk, is very useful in candy making as a flavor enhancer, adding richness to elements like caramel and fudge, and smoothness to ganache. The main differences between whipping and heavy cream (which is also, confusingly, sometimes called "heavy whipping cream") lie in their milk-fat content: whipping cream's is lower, around 30 to 36 percent; heavy cream's is 36 to 40 percent; while in the United Kingdom, "double cream" weighs in at a luxurious 48 percent. Whipping cream also often contains stabilizers and emulsifiers. Heavy cream, the purer product, is silkier, richer-tasting, and holds its body better when you whip it. Where cream is called for in our recipes, we mean American-style heavy cream, but in a pinch, whipping cream will do.

MOLTEN- CHOCOLATE PEANUT BARS

This is it: our favorite among all our artisan creations. Made with hand-crafted nougat, crowned with peanut-laden caramel, and drenched in good milk chocolate, it has everything we love in a candy bar—chewiness, nuttiness, sweet-saltiness, and that irresistible chocolate-caramel combo. Inspired by the world's bestselling candy bar, ours adds a double dose of vanilla for extra richness and the visual charm of vanilla-bean specks floating in soft white nougat.

MAKES
about
24
BARS

TIME NEEDED
about
1 HR 20 MIN

1 batch **Soft Vanilla Nougat** (page 103)

1 cup/220 g crunchy peanut butter (preferably organic)

1 batch **Basic-Batch Caramel** (page 109)

½ cup/55 g chopped peanuts (preferably blister peanuts)

1 batch **Tempered Milk Chocolate** (page 128)

1 Line two baking sheets with parchment paper or aluminum foil.

2 When preparing the nougat, add half the peanut butter, stir until the nougat is smooth, then scoop it from the bowl with a metal spoon and roll into 3-in/ 7.5-cm logs. (The shapes may be rough when the nougat is hot. Once it cools, it's easier to shape more precisely but will continue to be sticky.) Place the logs on one of the prepared baking sheets and set aside.

3 When the caramel has cooled for about 20 minutes, add the remaining peanut butter and stir until smooth. Stir in the chopped peanuts.

4 Using a metal spoon, scoop out enough caramel to form a layer about ½ in/ 12 mm thick on top of each log. Put the tray of logs in the refrigerator for about 10 minutes to set.

5 Have the tempered chocolate at 90°F/34°C. Using two dinner forks or chocolate dipping forks, dip each log into the chocolate. Shake off the excess chocolate, and slide logs onto the remaining baking sheet. Allow the chocolate to set by air-drying the bars with a small rotary fan for about 20 minutes or refrigerating for about 10 minutes. Serve at room temperature.

Store in an airtight container, a zip-top plastic bag, or plastic wrap in the refrigerator for 7 days, or in the freezer for 2 months.

EGYPTIAN NOUGAT BARS

MAKES
about

20 TO **24**
BARS

TIME NEEDED
about

1 HR **30** MIN

2 tbsp honey

1 cup/115 g slivered almonds, roasted (see page 69) and chopped

1 batch **Soft Chocolate Nougat** (page 101)

1 batch **Dark-Chocolate Caramel** (page 112), chilled in the refrigerator

1 batch **Tempered White Chocolate** (page 129)

As far back as the ancient Egyptians, people have relied on sugar for nourishment and pleasure. While their sugar took the form of honey, and chocolate was still unknown to them, the Egyptians were the first to make confections with foamed egg whites, sugar, and nuts. Thanks, Egyptians! In the interest of progress, we've added caramel and chocolate, dark and white, to the mix.

1 Line two baking sheets with parchment paper, cover one with a baking rack, then set them aside.

2 Add the honey and almonds to the nougat and set aside.

3 Shape the chilled caramel into 3-in/7.5-cm logs and place them on the baking rack.

4 Have the tempered chocolate at 90°F/34°C. Using a small paintbrush or pastry brush, paint each log with the chocolate. Allow them to cool about 20 minutes, then flip them over, chocolate-coated side down. Using a piping bag, pipe a 1-in/2.5-cm layer of chocolate nougat over each log.

5 Ladle the chocolate over each nougat-covered log and allow them to set for about 20 minutes at room temperature (a rotary fan aimed toward the bars speeds this up) or 10 minutes in the refrigerator. Serve at room temperature.

Store in an airtight container or a zip-top plastic bag at room temperature for 3 days, in the refrigerator for 2 weeks, or in the freezer for 2 months.

NUT 'N' NOUGAT BARS

One early candy bar had a catchy slogan touting the delicious simplicity of its three main ingredients: chocolate, nougat, and nuts. Our own bar piles airy nougat and crisp almonds on a salty pretzel under a blanket of milk chocolate. So for us, it's all about the chocolate, the nougat, the nuts, *and* the pretzel.

MAKES
about
24
PIECES

TIME NEEDED
about
1 HR

One 14-oz/400-g bag crunchy pretzels, preferably 3- to 4-in/ 7.5- to 10-cm twists

1 batch **Soft Vanilla Nougat** (page 103)

1 cup/115 g whole almonds, roasted (see page 69)

1 batch **Tempered Milk Chocolate** (page 128)

1 Line two baking sheets with parchment paper and set a baking rack on one of them. Put 20 to 24 pretzels on the baking rack.

2 Use a large piping bag or two large soupspoons to put a 2-in/5-cm scoop of nougat on each pretzel. Cover each scoop of nougat with 4 or 5 almonds.

3 Have the tempered chocolate at 90°F/34°C. Using a ladle, pour the chocolate over each pretzel-nougat-almond piece. Allow the chocolate to drip down the sides. Decorate the tops with one almond while the chocolate is still wet.

4 Allow the finished candy to dry at room temperature (a rotary fan aimed toward the bars speeds this up) for at least 20 minutes, or 10 minutes in the refrigerator. If desired, use a paintbrush to cover the bottom of each piece with chocolate. Serve at room temperature.

Store in an airtight container or a zip-top plastic bag at room temperature for 3 days, in the refrigerator for 2 weeks, or in the freezer for 2 months.

CHOCOLATE NOUGAT ○ CUPS ○

Along with marshmallows and divinity, nougat falls into the category of aerated confections, in which egg whites are cooked with hot sugar and fluffed up with air. Here, we've added dark chocolate to the fluffy nougat and encased it in crunchy milk-chocolate cups for a simple, classic candy treat.

MAKES
about

12
CUPS

TIME NEEDED
about

1 HR 15 MIN

1 batch **Tempered Milk Chocolate** (page 128)

1 batch **Soft Chocolate Nougat** (page 101)

1　Line a 12-cup muffin pan with cupcake liners.

2　Have the tempered chocolate at 90°F/34°C. With a small paintbrush or pastry brush, paint a thick layer of chocolate that reaches 1 to 1½ in/2.5 to 4 cm high up the inner sides of your cupcake liners and set them in the muffin pan. Refrigerate the pan for about 10 minutes to set the chocolate.

3　Spoon the nougat into the chilled, chocolate-coated cupcake liners, leaving a margin of chocolate along the top edge so the final coat of chocolate will adhere to it and seal the cups. Cover the nougat with that final layer of chocolate, and return the pan to the refrigerator for about 10 minutes. Serve at room temperature.

Store in an airtight container, a zip-top plastic bag, or plastic wrap at room temperature for 3 days, in the refrigerator for 2 weeks, or freezer for 2 months.

PB & CHOCOLATE CUPS

Child-like pleasure comes from taking something ordinary—like peanut butter, the everyday stuff of our school lunch boxes—and drenching it in special, dessert-quality chocolate. The resulting confection is both sturdy and sublime. We mix Vanilla-Bean Fudge with organic peanut butter to create a sweet, salty center you can take in several directions. For extra crunch, we add crispy rice. For a bit of PB & J nostalgia *and* layered flavors, make the PB & J Supreme Discs variation, which features chocolate, peanut butter, strawberry jam, and a topping of crunchy, salted peanuts. Of course, any of these can be made with dark chocolate—your choice.

MAKES
about

12
CUPS

TIME NEEDED
about

1 HR 20 MIN

1 batch **Vanilla-Bean Fudge** (page 118), made without optional pecans

1 cup/220 g crunchy peanut butter (preferably organic)

1 cup/25 g crispy rice cereal

1 batch **Tempered Milk Chocolate** (page 128)

1 Line an 8-in/20-cm square or round baking pan with buttered aluminum foil, and a baking sheet with parchment paper or foil. Have ready 12 cupcake liners and a 12-cup muffin pan.

2 Pour the fudge onto the prepared baking sheet, spoon the peanut butter on top, sprinkle the crispy rice atop that, and allow the entire mixture to cool to 110°F/42°C, as indicated on a candy thermometer. (If you are not using a thermometer and need an approximation, the fudge should feel no hotter than warm bath water.)

3 Once the peanut butter fudge has cooled to 110°F/42°C or below, stir it with two sturdy wooden spoons until it starts to thicken slightly—just a minute or two. Put it into the prepared baking pan and smooth it into an even layer, about 1½ in/4 cm thick.

4   Have the tempered chocolate at 90°F/34°C. With a small paintbrush or pastry brush, paint a thick layer of chocolate that reaches about 2 in/5 cm high up the inner sides of your cupcake liners. (You will fill the cups to about 1½ in/4 cm, which will leave a margin of chocolate along the top edge so the final coat of chocolate will adhere to it and seal the cups.) Set the liners in your muffin pan. Refrigerate for about 10 minutes to set the chocolate.

5   With a 2- or 3-in/5- or 7.5-cm biscuit cutter, cut thick discs (about 1½ in/4 cm tall) from the pan of prepared peanut butter fudge, and drop them into the chilled, chocolate-lined cups. Top with a layer of chocolate, return them to the refrigerator for 10 minutes, then serve.

Store in an airtight container, a zip-top plastic bag, or plastic wrap at room temperature for 3 days, 2 weeks in the refrigerator, or 2 months in the freezer.

Variation: PB & J Supreme Discs You will need 1 batch homemade Strawberry Jam (page 120) cooled to room temperature or ¾ cup/170 g store-bought jam, and 1 cup/115 g salted peanuts (preferably blister peanuts), roughly chopped.

Prepare the peanut butter fudge as directed but without the crispy rice. After placing a disc of peanut butter fudge in each cupcake liner, pour a thin layer of jam over the fudge discs. Add a thin layer of chopped peanuts, pressing them into the jam. Cover with another layer of tempered chocolate and refrigerate and serve as directed.

MILK-CHOCOLATE CUP-OF-FLUFFS

Can candy be too sweet? Not for us! The real delight of this sweet, sweet pairing of fluffy nougat and shredded coconut is what professional taste-testers call mouthfeel. The airy nougat softens, the coconut and almonds crunch, and the hefty milk chocolate shell melts and coats your palate with feel-good chocolate.

MAKES
about

24
CUPS

TIME NEEDED
about

1 HR

1 batch **Soft Vanilla Nougat** (page 103)

1 cup/95 g sweetened, shredded coconut, plus more to garnish

1/2 cup/60 g chopped, blanched, slivered almonds

1 batch **Tempered Milk Chocolate** (page 128)

1   Place 24 paper or foil cupcake liners in cupcake or muffin pans.

2   When preparing the nougat, add the coconut and almonds and set aside.

3   Have the tempered chocolate at 90°F/34°C. Using a small paintbrush or pastry brush, paint the inside of the cupcake liners with a thick coating of chocolate. Allow the chocolate cupcake liners to set in the refrigerator for 5 to 10 minutes. Fill each about half full with the coconut-nougat mixture, leaving a margin of chocolate along the top edge so the final coat of chocolate will adhere to it and seal the cups. Return the cups to the refrigerator for another 5 minutes, then top each with the finishing layer of chocolate and refrigerate again for 5 minutes to set. Decorate or sprinkle with shredded coconut. Remove from the muffin pan, and serve the cups with or without the liners.

Store in an airtight container, a zip-top plastic bag, or plastic wrap at room temperature for 2 days, in the refrigerator for 1 week, or freezer for 1 month.

Melty CHOCOLATE Minties

MAKES
about

24
DISCS

TIME NEEDED
about

1 HR 30 MIN

½ batch **Fondant** (page 106)

1 tsp peppermint extract, or
½ tsp peppermint oil (see
Shopping Resources Guide,
page 150)

24 **Candied Mint Leaves** (page 135;
optional)

1 batch **Tempered Dark Chocolate**
(page 126)

Aromatic peppermint meets earthy deep, dark chocolate in Susie's first artisan candy creation. The creamy fondant is an old-fashioned confection that takes some effort (slow sugar-cooking and paddling), but the work pays off in sweet dividends. We use a candied mint leaf garnish (best prepared a day ahead), though if you're pressed for time, skip that step.

1 Line two baking sheets with plastic wrap.

2 When preparing the fondant, add the peppermint extract after kneading the fondant into a paste. Knead further until the peppermint is completely absorbed. Adjust to taste.

3 Shape the fondant into 2-in/5-cm discs, place the discs on one of the prepared baking sheets, cover with plastic wrap, and refrigerate.

4 If you are making the mint leaves on the same day, prepare them using an oven temperature of 200°F/95°C.

5 Remove the fondant discs from the refrigerator and have the tempered chocolate at 90°F/34°C. Using a small pastry brush or paintbrush, paint one side of each disc with a thick layer of chocolate. Return the candy to the refrigerator.

6 Put a baking rack over the second baking sheet, remove the fondant discs from the refrigerator, and place them on the rack with the chocolate side down. Ladle chocolate over each disc, allowing the excess to drip through the rack onto the plastic-lined baking sheet. Place a mint leaf on top of each finished chocolate-coated disc, if desired. Refrigerate again for about 10 minutes to allow the chocolate to set, then serve.

Store in an airtight container or a zip-top plastic bag at room temperature for 3 days, in the refrigerator for 2 weeks, or in the freezer for 2 months.

chocolate BUTTER-TOFFEE SNAPS

Scientists tell us that the reason we love candy is that the marriage of sugar and fat charges the pleasure centers of our brains. We're all for it! This bar, just about pure sugar and pure butter, cheers us up mightily, especially once our crunchy toffee goes for a thick dunk in premium milk chocolate.

MAKES
about

16
PIECES

TIME NEEDED
about

1 HR **15** MIN

1 batch **Nutty Toffee** (page 115)

1 batch **Tempered Milk Chocolate** (page 128)

1 Line a baking sheet with parchment paper. As soon as you have finished preparing the toffee mixture, pour the hot (285°F/139°C) mixture out on the prepared baking sheet; allow it to cool for a few minutes. The still-soft toffee will be on its way to hardening. Score it with a 2-in/5-cm rectangular cookie cutter by pressing the cutter in as soon as the toffee is hard enough to hold the outline, then remove it. Allow the toffee to set completely, then cut the shapes out fully with the cutter and put each piece aside.

2 Have the tempered chocolate at 90°F/34°C. Dip the shaped toffee in the chocolate, shake off the excess, and place the finished bars on parchment paper or aluminum foil until ready to serve.

Store in an airtight container, a zip-top plastic bag, or plastic wrap at room temperature for 2 days, or for 2 weeks in the freezer.

CARAMEL PECAN TORTOISES

Inspired by a much-loved confection in the shape of a similar slow-moving reptile, we use pecans, caramel, and chocolate to produce jaunty tortoises with edible marzipan heads. We roast our pecans, mix up rich caramel, and use top-quality milk chocolate for the dipped "shells." The result is almost too cute to eat.

MAKES

20

TORTOISES

TIME NEEDED

about

2 HRS

3 cups/345 g pecan halves

1 batch **Milk-Chocolate Caramel** (page 113)

1 batch **Marzipan** (page 104) or ¾ cup/170 g store-bought marzipan

4 drops green food coloring

2 drops brown food coloring

1 batch **Tempered Milk Chocolate** (page 128)

1   Preheat the oven to 300°F/150°C/gas 2.

2   Line a baking sheet with parchment paper and roast the pecans until they're aromatic but not too brown, 10 to 15 minutes, and set aside.

3   As the caramel cools, line a baking sheet with parchment paper or aluminum foil. Place the pecan halves in groups of four on the baking sheet, arranging each group in an X-shaped formation.

4   Place the marzipan in a small bowl, apply the green and brown food coloring, and knead it in until the marzipan turns the desired reptilian color. Adjust as needed with more food coloring.

5   Mold 20 approximately 1½-in/4-cm, thin marzipan discs and place one over each point at which the four pecan halves intersect. Roll some of the remaining marzipan into small diamond-shaped heads and attach a head to each body.

6   Remove the caramel from the refrigerator and scoop a heaping 1 tbsp onto each tortoise body. Press all the pieces firmly together. Refrigerate the tortoises for about 10 minutes.

CONTINUED

7   Have the tempered chocolate at 90°F/34°C. Remove the tortoises from the refrigerator and pour 1 to 2 tbsp of chocolate over each caramel body. (The chocolate should drip over all the elements where they connect to the main body, which will help hold the tortoise together. If you like, dab eyes on each tortoise face with a chocolate-dipped toothpick.) Return the tray to the refrigerator for 10 to 15 minutes. Serve at room temperature.

Store in an airtight container, or a zip-top plastic bag at room temperature for 3 days, in the refrigerator for 2 weeks, or in the freezer for 2 months.

Chocolate and the Colonials

In 1765, the world's first dedicated chocolate factory was born in Dorchester, Massachusetts, out of a chance meeting between Dr. James Baker and a penniless Irishman, John Hannon, who knew how to mill cocoa beans on a commercial scale. Until then, individual apothecary shops had ground, sweetened, and mixed their own chocolate for customers who drank it for their health. The enterprising Baker and Hannon turned a sawmill on the Neponset River into a hugely successful grinding operation that spread the love—eventually becoming Baker's Chocolate, now owned by Kraft.

Notable chocolate-loving Americans included Thomas Jefferson, who so believed in its benefits that he wrote to John Adams in 1785, "The superiority of chocolate, both for health and nourishment, will soon give it the same preference over tea and coffee in America which it has in Spain." While that never quite happened, Baker's Chocolate has been in continuous operation since its opening, and has made its way into many American-made chocolate cakes and pans of fudge.

CHAPTER 3

BITS & BITES WE LOVE

A Few Delicious Extras

Here, we sneak in recipes that don't fit our definition of a candy bar—an all-in-one-piece proposition, often layered, and usually drenched in chocolate—but that we can't bear to leave out in the cold. We're thinking mostly of things that would fall in the "movie candy" category—because really, what would movies be (at home or in a theater) without those heart-melting mints and chews and other bite-size sweets? Please! Consider, too, how nice it is, when you're entertaining, to pass a bowl of small candies with dessert, or to tuck a couple on each saucer as you pass out coffee. There may be other times when you yourself want a bite of chocolate-caramel or a few mint buttons, instead of a whole bar. Read on.

We love the resolute chewiness of these. Because we're both such caramel fiends, and so crazy about great milk chocolate and dark chocolate, we incorporate extra-rich dark chocolate into our caramel before the milk-chocolate dip.

MAKES
about

36
PIECES

TIME NEEDED
about

1 HR 20 MIN

1 batch **Dark-Chocolate Caramel** (page 112)

1 batch **Tempered Milk Chocolate** (page 128)

1   Line a baking sheet with parchment paper.

2   Refrigerate the caramel until firm, for about 20 minutes (rather than 1 hour called for in the recipe). Use a small spoon to scoop out bite-size balls of caramel, put them on the prepared baking sheet, then roll each between the palms of your hands to smooth them out. (This is a messy job best done when wearing vinyl or latex gloves.) Return the balls to the sheet.

3   Have the tempered chocolate at 90°F/34°C. Using two small spoons or chocolate dipping forks, dip the balls in the tempered chocolate, shake off the excess, then return to the baking sheet. Allow the finished bites to harden at room temperature (a rotary fan aimed toward the bites speeds this up) for about 20 minutes or in the refrigerator for 10 minutes. Serve at room temperature.

Store in an airtight container or a zip-top plastic bag at room temperature for 3 days, in the refrigerator for 2 weeks, or in the freezer for 2 months.

CRUNCHY chocolate MINT BUTTONS

MAKES
36
PIECES

TIME NEEDED
about
1 HR **30** MIN

1 cup/115 g slivered almonds

½ batch **Fondant** (page 106)

1 tsp peppermint extract, or ½ tsp peppermint oil (see Shopping Resources Guide, page 150)

1 batch **Tempered Dark Chocolate** (page 126)

Lots of our candy-loving friends, not to mention our husbands, can get a bit irrational concerning chocolate and mint. For them, no other flavor sparks chocolate the way mint does, and vice versa. Don't even try to argue. Though *our* tastes range more widely (especially toward the caramel-nougat end of things), we totally get the point, above all when we're in the roaring darkness of the multiplex, in a mood for movie sweets. And because we *do* understand, we've come up with a way to drench peppermint-fondant buttons in fabulously dark choco-late. For a bit of crunch, we've also incorporated roasted almond bits into our buttons.

1. Line a baking sheet with parchment paper and set aside.

2. On a second baking sheet, roast the almonds at 350°F/180°C/gas 4 for about 10 minutes. Allow them to cool as you prepare the fondant, adding the peppermint extract to it at the same time you add the vanilla and salt called for in the recipe.

3. Using a small spoon, scoop up about 1 tbsp of the fondant, add several nut pieces to it and roll it into a ball between your palms. Put the balls, or buttons, on the prepared baking sheet, cover them with plastic wrap, and refrigerate.

4. Have the tempered chocolate at 90°F/34°C. Remove the buttons from the refrigerator and, using two small spoons or chocolate dipping forks, dunk each button into the chocolate, shake off the excess, and return it to the baking sheet. Allow the chocolate to set for 10 minutes in the refrigerator, then serve.

Store in an airtight container or a zip-top plastic bag at room temperature for 3 days, in the refrigerator for 2 weeks, or in the freezer for 2 months.

Chocolate Taffy

This recipe reminds us of long-ago October nights spent rushing from house to house untwisting the paper ends of delicious candy chews. For lots of deep, rich taste in addition to chewiness, we melt the best dark chocolate; mix it with corn syrup, vanilla, and salt; and roll it out like pie dough. Easy! It's also what we use to make Dark-Chocolate Flowers (page 132).

MAKES
about

2½
CUPS
(700 G)

TIME NEEDED
about

20 MIN

3 cups/465 g finely chopped high-quality dark chocolate

¾ cup/180 ml corn syrup

1 tsp vanilla extract

½ tsp salt

1 Melt the chocolate in a stainless-steel bowl over a pan of simmering water or the top portion of a double boiler. Stir in the corn syrup, vanilla, and salt. Remove from the heat and allow the mixture to cool to room temperature, stirring occasionally. The chocolate should come together with the consistency of pie dough and become more flexible as you work with it.

2 Place the mixture on a work surface covered with parchment paper and roll ¼ in/6 mm thick. Shape into a disc, then form into 6-in/15-cm logs. (If it's too soft to hold its shape, chill it for about 20 minutes and it will mold more easily.) Serve at room temperature.

Wrap each log individually in plastic wrap and store them in an airtight container or a zip-top plastic bag at room temperature for 7 days, in the refrigerator for 1 month, or in the freezer for 6 months.

CHOCOLATE SCALLOPS

There's something pleasing about chocolate molded into recognizable shapes, beginning with Easter bunnies and Thanksgiving turkeys. Our scallops feature milk-chocolate truffle creams and bits of roasted hazelnut encased in milk and white chocolate. You will need two madeleine cookie pans (see Shopping Resources Guide, page 150) to form the scallops.

MAKES
about

24
PIECES

TIME NEEDED
about

1 HR 20 MIN

½ batch **Tempered White Chocolate** (page 129)

½ batch **Tempered Milk Chocolate** (page 128)

½ cup/60 g roasted hazelnut pieces (see page 69; optional)

1 batch **Hazelnut-Chocolate Ganache** (variation, page 119), chilled

1 Have both tempered chocolates at 90°F/34°C. Using a small pastry brush or paintbrush, paint a generous amount of the white and milk chocolates in a mottled pattern in each cavity of the madeleine pan. Refrigerate for 10 minutes, then remove the pan from the refrigerator. Add the extra hazelnuts to the ganache (if using).

2 With a small spoon, scoop out enough ganache to smooth over the chocolate in the cookie cavities, leaving a shallow margin at the top. Pour just enough—about 2 tbsp—white or milk chocolate (or a mottled pattern of both) to cover the ganache. Shake the pan to encourage the top covering of chocolate to drip down and connect with the bottom layer, forming a seal. Refrigerate until the chocolate hardens, about 15 minutes.

3 Remove the pan from the refrigerator, turn it upside-down, and tap it over a work surface. The chocolate scallops should tumble out. If they don't, put the cookie sheet in the freezer for another 20 minutes, then try again. Serve at room temperature.

Store in an airtight container or a zip-top plastic bag in the refrigerator for 7 days or in the freezer for 2 months.

RAISINS IN THE DARK

Chocolate-covered raisins are a natural confection with excellent antioxidant properties. Commercial chocolate-covered raisins often have a smooth shape and sheen made possible by an enrobing machine. Here, our raisins are lavished with dark chocolate and retain their characteristic rumpled shapes.

MAKES
about

3 TO 4
CUPS
(600 TO 800 G)

TIME NEEDED
about

50 MIN

2 cups/340 g raisins

1 batch **Tempered Dark Chocolate**
(page 126)

1 Line a baking sheet with parchment paper or aluminum foil and set aside. Put about ½ cup/85 g raisins in a colander.

2 Have the tempered chocolate at 90°F/34°C. Hold the colander above the chocolate and ladle chocolate over the first batch of raisins. Toss them lightly as the chocolate drips out the bottom, then shake them out of the colander onto the prepared baking sheet. Repeat with the remaining raisins. Allow the chocolate to harden at room temperature (a rotary fan aimed toward the raisins speeds the process) for 20 minutes, or in the refrigerator for about 10 minutes. Serve at room temperature.

Store in an airtight container or a zip-top plastic bag at room temperature for 3 days, in the refrigerator for 2 weeks, or in the freezer for 2 months.

Southerners and their sugar! Susie's sister Libby, an unapologetic Kentucky sugar fiend, used to adore candy corn and eat it year-round, no matter how stale the left-over Halloween bags might have grown in the discount bin at the drugstore. For some reason, Libby called it Corn Candy, which fits our handcrafted version, dependent on corn syrup for its smoothness. We've made it sweet enough for Southerners and perhaps a few fiendish Northerners, too.

MAKES
about

24
PIECES

TIME NEEDED
about

1 HR 30 MIN

½ batch **Fondant** (page 106)
Orange and yellow food coloring

Refrigerate the fondant for about 20 minutes, then separate it into three batches. Apply a few drops of orange food coloring to the first batch and knead it into the fondant to make the right shade of Halloween orange. Repeat the process using yellow food coloring on the second batch to create a contrasting bright yellow. Leaving the third batch white, assemble the classic candy corn triangles, with a plump ball of orange fondant on the bottom, a smaller ball of white in the center, and a small ball of yellow on the top. Dip your finger in water and rub the pieces lightly, then press them together to form the triangular shape. Allow the finished candies to set in the refrigerator for about 20 minutes, then serve at room temperature.

Store in an airtight container or a zip-top plastic bag at room temperature for 3 days, in the refrigerator for 2 weeks, or in the freezer for 2 months.

CHAPTER 4
DREAM BARS

Healthier, Spicier, Sexier

Who says candy can't be good for you? It is if you make it so. Health-happy sweets are a hot trend in the candy biz. We focus on antioxidant-rich dark chocolate, which we've mentioned before but now celebrate in delicious concoctions called barks. These simple bars start with great-for-you walnuts, citrus peel, dried cherries, or other healthful bits suspended in deep, dark chocolate. That's it. Which means they're naturally lower in fat and sugar than many other candy bars, yet packed with the taste you crave in candy.

Barks showcase the natural contrast between light brown, roasted nuts and dark, cocoa-rich chocolate. Few rules exist for making chocolate bark, so you can be very creative with it. You will need to temper your chocolate, which is time-consuming, but there are ways to cheat if that process seems a burden (see Tempering: Too Much Trouble?, page 128). Within this section of recipes, we offer two different techniques for creating artful designs in the chocolate: One is to arrange nuts, dried fruits, and seeds, then pour tempered chocolate over them; the other is to pour tempered chocolate, allow it to harden a little, then arrange the add-ins in patterns on top

of that. It might be worth some trial and error to see which method you prefer. We'll start with a simple, basic bark, then move on to the more stylized and decorative varieties.

Most studies suggest that a 1-oz/28-g bar of very dark chocolate daily is a tonic for the cardio-vascular system. This finding is embraced by doctors and nutritionists around the world. We'll show you how to get creative with your healthy daily dose—to fill that dark-chocolate heaven, for instance, with nuts or fruits arranged in artful patterns, like flowers, or interesting abstract shapes. Also in this chapter, we'll talk about more ways to spice up your chocolate with flavors that have recently hit the food world hard. As you'll see in our recipes, the savor of green tea, for instance, pairs beautifully with chocolate, as do tarragon and chipotle.

Issues of health and popular taste aside, there are bars only you can imagine, those that mix up things you love the way ice-cream stores swirl in custom toppings. Picture a peanut butter and chocolate cup—with a layer of coconut, straw-berry jam, or crushed almond toffee. Imagine a thick, cookie-layered bar—with crispy rice or a drenching of deep, dark chocolate. If you've ever wished that your favorite bar had one more flavor note or extra bit of crunch, here's your chance to make it perfect with our Mix-&-Match Chart. You can pick and choose from the options as easily as spooning sprinkles from a dish.

We'll celebrate whimsy by giving you a few of our own improvised dream bars, selecting from among the many good ones we have cooked up in our kitchens, like Black & Pink Pepper-Caramel Cookie Bars or Choc-o-Nilla Nougat. It's fun to play around with tastes and textures, translating a particular ice cream or even a cocktail into a novel candy featuring citrus bits, handmade marshmallow, maple syrup, or liqueurs. You might think, by that point, that we'd gotten a bit far afield from the subject of chocolate and health, and you'd be right!

Every candy bar should be a private symphony of texture, taste, and pleasure. If you like crunch, why shouldn't your caramel bar have nuts and cookie crisps inside it? If you prefer silkiness, can't your soft nougat bar be layered with a smooth inner tier of nut-free fudge? Or how about a stream of caramel ribbon in a milk-chocolate shell? Inventing your own bars becomes irresistible as you improve your candy-making skills. We hope our examples will inspire yours, and give you a sense of the almost limitless possibilities that await you now that you know your way around a candy bar.

BASIC MIXED-NUT BARK

Among the most delicious yet easiest to make of all the barks, this one pairs the roasted sweetness of oven-browned nuts with slightly bitter dark chocolate amid a sprinkling of salt.

Line a baking sheet or two 8-in/20-cm cake pans with parchment paper. Combine all the nuts in a medium bowl and set aside about ½ cup/60 g of the mixed nuts to use as decoration. Have the tempered chocolate at 90°F/34°C and stir in the nuts and salt. Pour the chocolate and nuts onto the prepared baking sheet, spreading the bark so that it is about 1 in/2.5 cm thick. Arrange the reserved nuts on the top of the chocolate to create a pattern or design. Allow the bark to harden at room temperature for 30 minutes or in the refrigerator for about 15 minutes. To serve, remove the bark from the parchment and break it into pieces.

Store in an airtight container or a zip-top plastic bag at room temperature for 7 days, in the refrigerator for 3 weeks, or in the freezer for 6 months.

Variation: Quick Basic Bark Instead of tempering the chocolate, simply melt it over a water bath or very slowly in the microwave (see Is Chocolate Microwavable?, page 92), add all of the nuts and the salt, then spread the bark on the prepared baking sheet to set. Store in the refrigerator until ready to serve so the chocolate doesn't develop fat bloom. (See Tempering: Too Much Trouble?, page 128.)

Roasting Nuts

Ten minutes in a 350°F/180°C oven will bring out the natural oils and sweet aromas of the nuts we love most for candy fillings: peanuts, walnuts, pecans, cashews, pistachios, hazelnuts, macadamias, and pine nuts. Spread whole nuts on a baking sheet, and bake them until they're light brown and fragrant, about 10 minutes. Cool them at room temperature, and they're ready to press into service.

MAKES
about

24
PIECES

TIME NEEDED
about

40 MIN

½ cup/60 g broken cashews, roasted and salted

½ cup/60 g broken almonds, roasted and salted

½ cup/60 g broken walnuts, roasted and salted

½ cup/60 g broken shelled pistachios, roasted and salted

1 batch **Tempered Dark Chocolate** (page 126)

½ tsp sea salt (preferably coarse)

CANDIED MINT & CITRUS ZEST BARK

MAKES
about

24
PIECES

TIME NEEDED
about

1 HR 40 MIN

1 batch **Candied Mint Leaves**
(page 135)

1 batch **Candied Citrus** (page 136)

1 batch **Tempered Dark Chocolate**
(see page 126)

Lemon often meets mint in Middle Eastern and Mediterranean cuisine. Think of *limonana*, Israel's ubiquitous summer drink, which blends mint leaves, fresh-squeezed lemon juice, and ice. The combination of two such strongly aromatic notes also works well with dark chocolate, its bittersweet flavor a perfect complement to their acidic tang. And mint and citrus are healthful! Those dark-green leaves hold vitamins A, C, and B_{12}; those golden fruits have lots of C, along with potassium, calcium, and antioxidants. Both supply phytonutrients—plant-derived chemicals with disease-fighting powers—but citrus zest (the outermost, colored layer of the peel), which we call for here, has even more than the fruit. For best results, prepare the candied citrus zest and mint leaves and allow them to dry out in an unheated oven overnight before use.

1 Line a baking sheet or two 8-in/20-cm cake pans with parchment paper. Place the mint and citrus on top, reserving about 10 pieces for the garnish.

2 Have the tempered chocolate at 90°F/34°C. Pour ½ in/12 mm chocolate over the baking sheet, then decorate the top with the reserved candied pieces. Allow the chocolate to harden either at room temperature for 20 minutes or in the refrigerator about 10 minutes. When the chocolate is fully set, break the bark into pieces and serve.

Store in an airtight container or a zip-top plastic bag at room temperature for 1 week, in the refrigerator for 1 month, or in the freezer for 6 months.

MEDLEY OF Sesame & Sunflower BARK

MAKES
about

24
PIECES

TIME NEEDED
about

40 MIN

1 cup/130 g white sesame seeds

1/2 cup/70 g black sesame seeds

2 cups/230 g sunflower seeds

1 batch **Tempered Dark Chocolate**
(page 126)

The crunch of toasted seeds works magic in smooth, rich chocolate. Arranged in patterns on bark, these toasty bits add eye appeal too. Here, we start with white and black sesame, not just for the black's exotic looks but for the extra calcium and fiber in its hull. Meatier sunflower seeds give our add-ins more—and different—texture, and also up the content of vitamin E and assorted minerals.

1 Line a baking sheet or two 8-in/20-cm cake pans with parchment paper. Combine all the seeds in a bowl, and set aside about 1/2 cup/65 g to use as decoration.

2 Have the tempered chocolate at 90°F/34°C. Stir the remaining seeds into the chocolate. Pour the chocolate mixture onto the prepared baking sheet, spreading the bark to no more than 3/4 in/2 cm thick, if you want a bark that's easy to bite. With a small spoon, arrange the reserved seeds on top of the chocolate to create a pattern. Allow the bark to harden at cool room temperature for 30 minutes or in the refrigerator for about 15 minutes. To serve, remove the bark from the parchment and break into pieces.

Store in an airtight container or a zip-top plastic bag at room temperature for 2 weeks, in the refrigerator for 1 month, or in the freezer for 6 months.

CHIPOTLE CHOCOLATE COINS

MAKES
about
24
PIECES

TIME NEEDED
about
1 HR 10 MIN

2 tbsp chipotle pepper powder

2 tbsp cayenne pepper or paprika

1 batch **Tempered White Chocolate** (page 129)

1 batch **Tempered Dark Chocolate** (page 126)

Chocolate's long-standing association with chiles dates back to the ancient Mayan civilization and the Olmec of Mesoamerica, who spiced cocoa with chile peppers. Today, as chefs get ever more adventurous with taste pairings, chiles' spicy powers are valued in applications from soups and stews to desserts. Chipotle, a smoked, dried jalapeño, adds smokiness to the pepper heat, and both enhance a fruity dark chocolate's flavors. Capsaicin, the chemical compound that puts the heat in hot peppers, can reportedly lower blood sugar, clear nasal congestion, reduce inflammation, and lower the risk of some cancers. But our creation brings some sinfulness to the table in the form of white chocolate.

1 Line a baking sheet or two 8-in/20-cm cake pans with parchment paper. Mix the chipotle pepper powder and cayenne together in a small bowl. Using a small spoon, draw designs with the mixed powders on the baking sheet.

2 Have the tempered white chocolate at 90°F/34°C. Spoon the white chocolate over the powder designs, rounding the outer edge to create coin-shaped candy discs. Refrigerate to allow the discs to set.

3 Have the tempered dark chocolate at 90°F/34°C. Remove the baking sheet from the refrigerator and pour the dark chocolate about 1 in/2.5 cm thick over the white-chocolate discs. Return the pan to the refrigerator for at least 10 minutes or until ready to serve.

Store in an airtight container or a zip-top plastic bag in the refrigerator for 3 days, or in the freezer for 2 months.

CLASSIC DARK-CHOCOLATE TRUFFLES

By incorporating very dark chocolate, no extra sugar, and a lighter version of our ganache recipe, these truffles deliver high health benefits in bite-size offerings. A classic French confection, they're named after precious truffle mushrooms, which also have a dark, irregular shape.

Line two baking sheets with parchment paper. Refrigerate the ganache for 30 minutes. Melt the dark chocolate over a water bath until smooth. Remove the ganache from the refrigerator, scoop out small, round pieces of it with a soupspoon or melon baller, and place on the prepared baking sheets. Dip the pieces into the melted chocolate and place them on the sheets to set, about 5 minutes. While they're still a little soft, roll them in the cocoa powder and return them to the baking sheets. Refrigerate for 20 minutes. Serve at room temperature.

Store in an airtight container or a zip-top plastic bag in the refrigerator for 4 days or in the freezer for 2 months.

MAKES
about

40
TRUFFLES

TIME NEEDED
about

1 HR 30 MIN

1 batch **Light Chocolate Ganache** (variation, page 119), using high-quality dark chocolate

2 cups/310 g high-quality dark chocolate, finely chopped

1/2 cup/50 g unsweetened cocoa powder, sifted

One Dark Ounce:
MAKING THE MOST OF YOUR DAILY DOSE

For those of us used to powering down the chocolate, 1 ounce (about 28 grams) may not seem like much. But look at it this way: You hereby have permission to eat chocolate, guilt-free, every day! Of course—and wouldn't you know it—that license comes with some restrictions. The chocolate must be dark (with a minimum of 60 percent cocoa content) and free of hydrogenated or partially hydrogenated fats, and you can't drink it with milk, which seems to nix dark chocolate's antioxidant value to the body. Some days, you might want to down your dose in the form of cocoa nibs (see What Are Cocoa Nibs?, page 35), which blend beautifully, for example, into dairy-free fruit smoothies. And by all means, try ultra-healthful products such as CocoaVia from Mars, Inc., and Acticoa from Barry Callebaut, which are specially processed to maintain maximum amounts of the flavanols and other super-nutrients in dark chocolate.

Chopping Chocolate

Chocolate melts more uniformly when chopped into very small pieces. Thin bars are easy to chop, but chocolate is often sold in big blocks. Here are the best approaches to dealing with these:

• Use a serrated knife (bread knife). This gives you more traction against the chocolate and also works like a grater.

• Chop a big chunk of chocolate starting at a corner of the block. Don't start in the middle, where you'll find more resistance.

• Try a chocolate chipper. Available in gourmet kitchenware stores, this gadget is similar to an ice pick.

Green-Tea TRUFFLES

MAKES
about

24
TRUFFLES

TIME NEEDED
about

1 HR

2 cups/310 g finely chopped premium white chocolate

1½ cups/360 ml heavy cream

2 green-tea bags

½ tsp salt

1 tsp vanilla extract

About ¼ cup/55 g *matcha* (Japanese green-tea powder; see Shopping Resources Guide, page 150)

¾ cup/70 g powdered sugar

½ cup/15 g crispy rice cereal, crushed

We don't often call on white chocolate, but when we do, we've got our reasons. In this case, we use it with creamy ganache and sweetened *matcha*, or green-tea powder. The tea's subtle sharpness reins in the sweetness of the white chocolate, and its natural color adds an unexpected soft green hue. As for tea's antioxidant properties, there may not be enough of the green here to protect you from cancer and heart disease, but what is there can't hurt! This recipe was inspired by Mary's Chocolates of Belgium, experts in high-quality chocolates with artful designs.

1 In a double boiler, partially melt the white chocolate over simmering water until it's semiliquid but still lumpy. Place the cream, tea bags, and salt in a heat-proof measuring cup and microwave for 1 minute. (Alternatively, heat these ingredients in a small saucepan just until they simmer, then cool for 1 minute.) Remove the tea bags. In a medium bowl, stir together the cream mixture and the melted chocolate. Add the vanilla. Keep stirring until the mixture smooths into a well-blended ganache.

2 Cool the ganache in the refrigerator for at least 30 minutes.

3 With two spoons, scoop 1-in/2.5-cm balls of the ganache onto a baking sheet. Roll the balls with your hands into smooth, uniform shapes. Chill if necessary.

4 Sift the matcha and powdered sugar together in a small bowl. Mix in the cereal. Dip each ganache ball into the matcha mixture and shake off the excess. Serve at room temperature.

Store in an airtight container or a zip-top plastic bag in the refrigerator for 4 days or for 2 months in the freezer.

TARRAGON & WASABI BARS

These bars play up harmonies among unusual mates, including herbs you might have relegated to savory foods: tarragon, wasabi, peas! Within an outer coating of milk chocolate, tarragon's aromatic sweetness balances a dark-chocolate layer, the crunch of dried peas, and the unmistakable bite of wasabi paste. Aside from taste, chocolate offers antioxidants while the tarragon adds vitamins and minerals. The wasabi, made from Japanese horseradish, is just for fun and an extra zesty kick.

MAKES
about

30
PIECES

TIME NEEDED
about

1HR

½ batch **Tempered Milk Chocolate** (page 128)

1 tsp wasabi paste

1 tsp salt

½ cup/80 g dried peas (see Shopping Resources Guide, page 150)

1 tbsp dried tarragon

1 batch **Tempered Dark Chocolate** (page 126)

1 Line a baking sheet or two 8-in/20-cm cake pans with parchment paper and refrigerate.

2 Have the tempered milk chocolate at 90°F/34°C. Stir the wasabi paste into the milk chocolate. Add the salt to the milk chocolate. Remove the prepared baking sheet from the refrigerator and pipe or spoon small discs—about 2 in/5 cm wide—of the milk chocolate onto them, about 1 in/2.5 cm apart. (These should thicken quickly on the cold pan.) Press the peas into the milk chocolate, sprinkling tarragon around them to resemble flower petals. Refrigerate the baking sheet for at least 10 minutes.

3 Have the tempered dark chocolate at 90°F/34°C. Flip the discs over on the parchment and pour the dark chocolate to cover them, about 1 in/2.5 cm thick. Add additional peas on top, if desired. Allow the bark to set further in the refrigerator for at least 30 minutes, then remove from the parchment and present on a platter.

Store in an airtight container or a zip-top plastic bag at room temperature for 7 days, in the refrigerator for 2 weeks, or in the freezer for 6 months.

Variation: Quick Flower Bark Follow the method as directed but omit the milk chocolate and wasabi. Melt the dark chocolate in a water bath or microwave rather than tempering it. Lay the pea-and-tarragon patterns directly onto the parchment and secure them with a small amount of melted dark chocolate. Allow the patterns to set, then pour the rest of the melted dark chocolate over them. Keep the finished bark in the refrigerator until serving.

Lucky Kit Kats

During a recent trip to Japan, Susan discovered Kit Kats in exotic flavors like chili, green tea, and cherry blossom on the shelves of Tokyo and Kyoto markets. Investigating these intriguing products, she learned they're manufactured at different times of year and given as good-luck gifts, for graduation, special birthdays, and promotions. The similarity between the bar's name and the Japanese phrase *kitto katsu*—which roughly translates to "You will surely win!"—inspires parents to send children to school with a Kit Kat as a lucky charm. Senior high-school students get them, too, before taking university entrance exams. To meet the demand, novel flavors of Japanese Kit Kats have been released for short periods of time: maple syrup, melon, vanilla bean, grape, apple, banana, caramel, kiwi fruit, azuki, and yuzu. Depending on what's available at the moment, you can find these and other wondrous variations through online sources such as Amazon.com.

BLACK & PINK PEPPER- CARAMEL COOKIE BARS

MAKES
about

24
BARS

TIME NEEDED
about

1 HR 40 MIN

1 batch **Very-Vanilla Sugar Cookies**
(page 123)

¼ cup/50 g black peppercorns,
ground, plus more for seasoning

¼ cup/50 g pink peppercorns,
ground, plus peppercorns for
garnish

1 batch **Basic-Batch Caramel**
(page 109)

Salt

1 batch **Tempered Milk Chocolate**
(page 128)

The quest for pepper drove the spice trade for centuries. Native to Asia, this fiery berry traveled to ancient Greece and Rome, often teaming up with sweets along the way. According to *La Rousse Gastronomique*, the ripe berries range in color from warm pink to crimson red, but they're harvested at different stages of maturity. The early pinks are dried, retain their bright color, and impart a mild flavor. The mature reds turn black when dried and deliver the full firepower we associate with freshly ground black pepper. We've blended a small dose of pink and black peppercorns in homage to this plant's ability to ramp up the flavors of food, both sweet and savory.

1 When preparing the sugar cookie dough, add the ground black and pink peppercorns at the end, then form the dough into 3-in/7.5-cm logs, and bake as directed. When preparing the caramel, add ½ tsp salt to it.

2 Transfer the cookies to a baking sheet lined with parchment paper. Pour a thin layer of caramel over each cookie and allow it to drip down the sides. Season with salt and more ground black peppercorns. Refrigerate the cookies.

3 Have the tempered chocolate at 90°F/34°C. Remove the cookies from the refrigerator and dip each into the chocolate, shake off the excess, and return them to the baking sheet. While they're still wet, decorate them lightly with pink peppercorns (one little peppercorn packs a lot of heat!). Allow them to set at room temperature (a rotary fan aimed at the cookies speeds the process) for 20 minutes or in the refrigerator for about 10 minutes. Serve at room temperature.

Store in an airtight container or a zip-top plastic bag at room temperature for 3 days or in the freezer for 2 months. (This bar will lose its crunch if stored in the refrigerator.)

ORANGE-CHOCOLATE COOKIE CRUNCH BARS

MAKES
about

24
BARS

TIME NEEDED
about

2 HR **20** MIN

1 batch **Chocolate Sugar Cookies** (page 121)

2 tbsp orange juice

1 tbsp orange zest

1 batch **Orange-Brandy Caramel Sauce** (page 143)

1 batch **Tempered Dark Chocolate** (page 126)

1 batch **Candied Citrus** (optional; page 136), using only oranges

We take oranges for granted today, but once, they were exotic treasures that miraculously appeared from far-off, sunny lands or were grown in the hothouses of the royal and rich. We still prize their bright, fresh flavor, especially in desserts, and layer it here with orange-infused brandy, caramel, and crisp cookies.

1. Line two baking sheets with parchment paper and put a baking rack on one.

2. Prepare the sugar cookie dough and add the orange juice and orange zest at the same time you add the vanilla. Shape into 3-in/7.5-cm logs, and bake as directed.

3. Put the cookies on the baking rack and drizzle each one with a thick layer of caramel sauce. Allow the sauce to drip down the sides of the cookies.

4. Have the tempered chocolate at 90°F/34°C. Dip each caramel-coated cookie in the chocolate, remove with two dinner forks or chocolate dipping forks, shake off the excess, and put on the remaining baking sheet. While the chocolate is still warm and sticky, arrange the candied citrus (if using) on top of the cookie bars. Let them dry at room temperature (a rotary fan pointed at them will speed the process) for 20 minutes, or refrigerate for 10 minutes. Serve at room temperature.

Store in an airtight container or a zip-top plastic bag at room temperature for 3 days or in the freezer for 2 months. (They will lose their crunch if stored in the refrigerator.)

Maple-NUT LOGS

Use pure maple syrup for this recipe, rather than the sweeter, ersatz pancake syrup you might find beside the maple syrup in the grocery store. While maple syrups are labeled with quality grades (in general, the darker they are, the more flavor they have), what matters here is a 100 percent pure product.

1 Line two baking sheets with parchment paper. When you pour the fondant into the bowl of an electric mixer to cool, add the maple syrup.

2 Spread the peanuts over one of the baking sheets and set aside. When the maple fondant is ready, form it into 3-in/7.5-cm logs. Spoon the caramel onto a work surface and smooth it out. Cut off 3-by-1-in/7.5-by-2.5-cm rectangles and wrap a piece of caramel around each maple-fondant log. Roll the logs in the peanuts and place on the remaining baking sheet. Serve at room temperature.

Store in an airtight container or a zip-top plastic bag in the refrigerator for 7 days, or in the freezer for 6 months.

Simple Variation: Omit the caramel layer and roll the maple fondant logs in the peanuts.

Extra-Sweet Variation: Use maple-coated or honey-coated peanuts.

MAKES
about

24
LOGS

TIME NEEDED
about

1 HR 40 MIN

½ batch **Fondant** (page 106)

3 tbsp pure maple syrup

2 cups/230 g peanuts, roasted (see page 69) and chopped

½ batch **Milk-Chocolate Caramel** (page 113)

ROCKY ROAD

Americans associate Rocky Road with chocolate ice cream swirled with marshmallows and nuts. But in England and Australia, it can be a milk-chocolate-and-marshmallow icing that's popular on cupcakes. This candy bar blends both versions of Rocky Road, which should satisfy sweet cravings in any English-speaking country.

MAKES
about

18
WEDGES

TIME NEEDED
about

1 HR 50 MIN

1 batch **Tempered Dark Chocolate** (page 126)

1 batch **Marshmallow** (page 100)

1 cup/115 g almonds, preferably Marcona, roasted (see page 69) and salted

1 batch **Milk-Chocolate Ganache** (page 119), melted

1   Line an 8-in/20-cm round cake pan with parchment paper.

2   Have the tempered chocolate at 90°F/34°C. Cut the marshmallow into 1-in/2.5-cm cubes and put about six of them in the prepared cake pan. Sprinkle in half of the almonds, and drizzle with about half of the ganache. Pour half of the dark chocolate over the marshmallows, nuts, and ganache. Arrange more marshmallow cubes, nuts, and swirls of ganache in the pan, and coat with the remaining dark chocolate. Allow the chocolate to set in the refrigerator for 20 minutes. Unmold the Rocky Road as you would a pan of fudge (see Flip Out, page 88). Use a hot knife to cut into wedges and serve.

Store in an airtight container or a zip-top plastic bag at room temperature for 2 weeks or in the freezer for 2 months. (Rocky Road doesn't store well in the refrigerator.)

Candy Sugar vs. Hidden Sugar

Not long ago, online food and wine magazine Zester Daily ran an editorial that moved both of us deeply. Written by professional baker Gesine Bullock-Prado, author of the book, *Sugar Baby*, it made an impassioned case for the conscious enjoyment of well-crafted sweets in an otherwise healthful, whole-foods diet. She pointed out that an inordinate number of commercially prepared and packaged foods (salad dressing, soup, yogurt, crackers, etc.) contain what she calls "sneaky" sugar, particularly in the form of high-fructose corn syrup that you'd never know was there. Yet when you eat these foods, you take in their extra sugar (and often fat) calories without the satisfaction of deliberately indulging your sweet tooth. In her view (and we agree—oh, do we!), it makes more sense to make your own straightforward, pure-ingredients soup and salad dressing, eat sensibly and well, and then top off this good behavior with a piece of candy you make yourself. As we've said elsewhere in this book, when you make it, you know exactly what's in it; you're not being penalized by stealth ingredients. Sure, you're splurging, but you've earned it, and in a form that you can taste: In other words, pure, healthful food plus hand-crafted sweets (not every day) equals conscious bliss.

CHOC-O-NILLA NOUGAT

Chocolate and vanilla were born together in the wild jungles of pre-Columbian Mexico. Then, as now, cacao trees grew in harmony with the shy little flowers of the vanilla orchid, and together, the two become a potent flavor team in the world of sweets. Here, in tribute to their age-old friendship, we take chocolate and vanilla nougat and pipe them side by side over a thin layer of luscious fudge.

MAKES
about

20
BARS

TIME NEEDED
about

1 HR 30 MIN

1 batch **Soft Vanilla Nougat** (page 103)

1/2 cup/80 g melted high-quality dark chocolate

1 batch **No-Fail Chocolate Fudge** (page 116)

Shaved chocolate, cocoa nibs, or fresh raspberries to garnish

1 Scoop out half the nougat into a separate bowl and stir in the melted chocolate. Now you have two nougat flavors, vanilla and chocolate. Place each in a piping bag fitted with matching tips (such as the star tip number 826; see Tips on Tips, page 141).

2 Remove the fudge from its pan by flipping it onto a cutting board. Slice the fudge into 2-by-3-in/5-by-7.5-cm rectangles or other shapes, then pipe matching bands of vanilla and chocolate nougat on top of the fudge slices. Garnish with shaved chocolate and serve at room temperature.

Store in an airtight container at room temperature for 3 days or freeze for up to 2 months. (These don't keep well in plastic wrap or in the refrigerator.)

Flip Out

To remove fudge easily from a baking pan, loosen the edges from the sides with a spatula tip or paring knife, being careful not to scratch the bottom of the pan. Cover the pan with a large cutting board (lightweight flexible cutting boards are perfect for this job). Pick up the pan with the cutting board on top, hold it firmly with one hand, and put your other hand over the cutting board. Quickly flip the pan. Place the cutting board on your work surface, and the fudge will fall out onto the board. Cut it as is, or flip it right-side-up to cut.

TART Cherry JUNGLE

MAKES
about

24
PIECES

TIME NEEDED
about

1 HR

This confection features dried cherries, which are filled with antioxidant properties and vitamins A and C. Our recipe takes a mix-and-match approach to its design, featuring a spectrum of possible colors, from pistachio-green to cashew-brown to wild cranberry-red.

1 cup/85 g dried tart cherries

Four or more of the following:

1 cup/115 g pistachios (shelled)

1/2 cup/60 g almonds

1/2 cup/45 g dried cranberries

1/2 cup/60 g dried hulled pumpkin seeds (also known as pepitas)

1/2 cup/60 g macadamia nuts

1 cup/115 g cashews

1/2 cup/75 g dried apricots, thinly sliced

1/2 cup/40 g candied lemon zest, roughly chopped

1 batch **Tempered Dark Chocolate** (page 126)

1   Line a baking sheet or two 8-in/20-cm cake pans with parchment paper. Arrange the cherries and your choice of nuts and dried fruits in your desired pattern, setting aside 1/2 cup for decoration.

2   Have the tempered chocolate at 90°F/34°C. Pipe or spoon a 1/2-in/12-mm layer of chocolate to cover the fruits and nuts and allow the chocolate to set for 20 minutes. Pour the remaining chocolate over them and add decorative nuts and fruits on top. Allow to cool for 20 minutes in the refrigerator. Break into pieces or serve whole at room temperature.

Store in an airtight container or a zip-top plastic bag at room temperature for 7 days, in the refrigerator for 2 weeks, or in the freezer for 6 months.

Is Chocolate Microwavable?

Chefs differ on whether it's advisable to melt chocolate in a microwave. The biggest problem is that chocolate burns easily, and it burns especially easily in a microwave, which distributes heat unevenly throughout food. The short answer is, yes, chocolate can be melted successfully in the microwave, but you need to take some precautions.

Put the chocolate in something microwave-safe, like a Pyrex bowl or measuring cup. Never use metal or aluminum foil!

On the lowest heat setting, microwave chocolate for no more than 30 seconds at a time. This is a cautious and slightly tedious approach, since you'll need to open the microwave and stir the chocolate, then zap it for 30 seconds several times before it actually melts. But this eliminates the otherwise likely possibility that the chocolate will burn.

Chicago: Historic Candy Town

Long known as a candy-making—and candy-eating—hub, Chicago was the host of the 1893 Columbian Exposition, the world's fair where Milton Hershey fell in love with German chocolate machines and switched his focus from caramel to chocolate. But other sweets firms, most notably Mars, arose in the Windy City, where the endless, freezing winters made for a long candy-making season in the days before refrigeration. Chicago's extensive railroad network, too, supplied ready transport to get perishable bars around the country fast. At one time or another, many well-known confectioners have operated here, including Brachs, DeMet's, Fannie May, and Curtiss. While some have closed or been absorbed by larger companies, other favorites are still around, among them Tootsie Roll, Blommer, Mars, and the upscale Vosges.

CHOCOLATE-DIPPED STRAWBERRIES

MAKES
about

24
PIECES

TIME NEEDED
about

40 MIN

24 large fresh strawberries or other fruit

1 batch **Tempered Dark Chocolate** (page 126)

Eat a ripe strawberry coated in dark chocolate and you get the health benefits of both. And the flavors! Each complements the other. Then, there's the pleasure of biting into the thick, crisp chocolate to meet the juicy fruit. But don't stop with strawberries. Pitted fresh cherries, peach slices, and bananas work wonderfully too, as do chewier options such as dried apricots and dried plums.

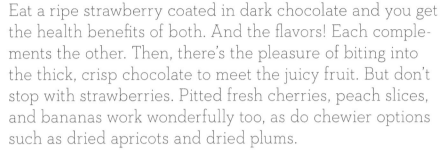

Line a baking sheet with parchment paper. Pierce each strawberry with a bamboo skewer or a dinner fork. Have the tempered chocolate at 90°F/34°C. Dip the strawberry into the chocolate, shake off the excess, then remove from the skewer or fork and place on the prepared baking sheet. Allow the chocolate to set on the dipped strawberries for 10 minutes in the refrigerator. Serve at room temperature.

Store in an airtight container or a zip-top plastic bag in the refrigerator for 3 days.

Variation: Quick-Dipped Fruit Fondue Instead of tempering the chocolate, prepare a batch of Milk-Chocolate Ganache (page 119) or Dark-Chocolate Ganache (see variation, page 119). Keep the ganache warm in a fondue pot, and allow guests to skewer and dip the fruit right out of the pot. Or, you can dip the fruit, then put it on a baking sheet lined with parchment and refrigerate until serving.

Hazelnut STRAWBERRY Jams

Even chocolate creators have their preferences. At Happy Chocolates, Susie's online chocolate boutique, a bonbon filled with hazelnut cream, milk chocolate, and fresh strawberry jam is by far her favorite. Here, the same sweet flavors are propped up by a layer of crunchy cookie.

MAKES
about
24
COOKIES

TIME NEEDED
about
2 HR 20 MIN

1 batch **Very-Vanilla Sugar Cookies** (page 123)

1 batch **Hazelnut-Chocolate Ganache** (variation, page 119)

1 tbsp Frangelico (hazelnut liqueur; optional)

1 tbsp dark rum (optional)

1 batch **Strawberry Jam** (page 120)

Fresh strawberry slices to garnish (optional)

1 Shape the sugar cookie dough into 2-in/5-cm discs and use the tip of a spoon to carve a round groove across the top of each cookie before it goes into the oven. Bake as directed. When preparing the ganache, add the Frangelico and rum (if using) with the cream.

2 Use a spoon to scoop a generous layer of ganache into the groove of each cookie. Spread more ganache thickly and smoothly on top of the cookies, then spoon a thin layer of jam over the ganache. Allow the cookies to set in the refrigerator for 20 minutes, decorate with fresh strawberry slices if desired, and serve at room temperature.

Store in an airtight container in the refrigerator for 2 days or in the freezer for 2 months.

CHAPTER 5
CANDY-BAR BASICS

Fundamental Recipes and Techniques

Candy bars may look like a complex proposition, but as with so many layered things (your winter wardrobe, *War and Peace*), they're more easily navigated in parts. Here's where we break it all down and tell you everything you need to know to make bars from simple to elaborate.

Candy bars consist of several layers, most hidden inside with an outside coating, usually chocolate. When you make bars, you work from the inside out, so in presenting our recipes, we do too. Most of the following recipes provide a key component for one of the bars listed in the previous chapters. A few give you variations or elements you need, if you want to build your own bar—see our Mix-and-Match Chart (page 99). Our key components include Fillings, Coatings, and Garnishes.

Fillings

Caramels, Creams (which include fondant, ganache, and fudge), Fluffs, Crunches, Cookies, and Jam

CARAMELS

Here, we're talking about the soft, pliant form of caramel in several variations, since specific candy bars call for caramel in different thicknesses and textures. We will save hard caramel (and *its* various incarnations) for our Crunches topic (following). With all our cooked sugar recipes, we take precautions by including in the ingredients a bowl of ice, which serves to cool off or shock the sugar when it reaches the desired color.

CRUNCHES

Things that *crunch* in candy bars delight us. As you bite into a smooth or creamy bar and hit that bit of crackle, you have to wonder what it is: Toasted nuts? Caramel chips? In our recipes, it might be one or both—that crumbly combo of sugar and nuts that Europeans call "praline." In fact, the terminology around crunches can be confusing. Some confectioners use "toffee" and "brittle" interchangeably, to denote a sugar-and-butter mix that has been heated and cooked until it has lost most of its moisture and gone cracking-hard. Some distinguish "caramel" and "toffee" by their ingredients, with caramel more often containing cream, toffee containing butter. We'd like to simplify things by dispensing with controversy altogether, so we'll call toffee and hard caramel brothers in the same family, and show you how to use them to add the right amount of crunch to your candy creations.

FUDGE

It just breaks our hearts to think about what a disservice mass production and a lot of little seaside tourist shops have done to fudge—transformed it from a hugely satisfying and well-worth-the-calories pleasure into something bland, waxy, and undeserving of the name! If you make it yourself, you can combine quality European butter, the best chocolate, and delicious heavy cream into something miraculous. And fudge is a great element for a Mix-and-Match bar. Use it as a base to top with a cookie, perhaps a dollop of caramel, an extra scatter of nuts, and—why not?—a coating of great dark chocolate.

FLUFFS

The secret to the airiness of these assorted creams and nougats (technically known as "aerated confections") is whipped egg whites. Paired with caramel, coconut, a crunchy cookie, or simply enveloped in good chocolate, fluffs lighten up the mix.

COOKIES

You may not connect cookies with your candy bars, but as you deconstruct many of your favorites, there they are. Cookies lend a welcome texture to a range of chewy, gooey elements, but their presence is structural, too: They hold up crucial softer layers, including caramels, nougats, and creams.

Coatings

Dark Chocolate, Milk Chocolate, White Chocolate, and Nuts

CHOCOLATE

To create beautiful, chocolate-coated candy bars, you can't just melt the chocolate and dip the bars. Or you can, but you might not like the results (see Tempering: Too Much Trouble?, page 128). For the most glossy appearance and best texture, you must temper or "precrystallize" the chocolate, or its natural cocoa butter and cocoa solids will separate and form blemishes, called fat bloom, on the surface of your bar. Tempering requires a candy or digital thermometer and a little patience as you heat, then cool, then heat the chocolate again. When the molecules align just right, you've got the perfect thick, smooth, shiny candy coating you need for any bar you want to make.

You can cover candy in dark, milk, or white chocolate. The proper temperatures vary slightly with the type of chocolate, so we've included instructions for each. In each case, for bigger chocolate-dipping jobs, you can increase the amount of chocolate and follow the same procedure.

An alternative to the careful process of tempering chocolate, of course, is to cover your candy bar in nuts and call it a day.

NUTS

A roll in a pile of roasted nuts—sliced, chopped, or even left whole—is one of the simplest possible finishes to a candy bar, yet one of the most satisfying, adding extra crunch and rich, toasty flavor. Nuts adhere especially well to fudge, but don't stop there. If you're a true nut fiend, try the nut-roll around a center of Chocolate Taffy (page 61), Marzipan (page 104), or Dark- or Milk-Chocolate Caramel (pages 112 and 113).

Mix-and-Match Chart Choose as many fillings as you like from category 1, sprinkle in an add-in or two (category 2), then finish up with the coating and/or garnish of your choice (categories 3 and 4).

FILLINGS

1 CARAMEL
Basic-Batch
Dark-Chocolate
Milk-Chocolate

1 COOKIES
Chocolate Sugar
Very-Vanilla Sugar
Brown Sugar–Crisps

1 CRUNCHES
Hard Caramel
Nutty Caramel
Crushed Praline Powder
Nutty Toffee
Mixed-Nut Toffee
Not-So-Nutty Toffee

1 FLUFFS
Marshmallow
Soft Vanilla Nougat
Soft Chocolate Nougat

1 FONDANT

1 FUDGE
No-Fail Chocolate
Old-Fashioned Chocolate
Vanilla-Bean
Maple
Milk-Chocolate

1 GANACHE
Milk-Chocolate
Dark-Chocolate
White-Chocolate
Hazelnut-Chocolate
Light Chocolate

1 MISCELLANY
Marzipan
Strawberry Jam

ADD-INS

2 FRUIT
Candied Citrus
raisins
dried apricots
dried plums
dried berries
dried cherries
coconut

2 NUTS
peanuts
walnuts
pecans
hazelnuts
almonds
macadamias
pistachios
nut butters

2 SEEDS
white sesame
black sesame
sunflower
pine nuts

2 SPICY THINGS
chipotle
cracked or ground peppercorns
saffron
green tea
mint
tarragon
ginger

COATINGS

3 NUTS
peanuts / walnuts / pecans / hazelnuts / almonds / macadamias / pistachios

3 TEMPERED CHOCOLATE
dark / milk / white

GARNISHES

4 CANDIED CITRUS

4 CANDIED MINT LEAVES

Marsh-mallow

Named after the spongy mallow plant that grows in marsh-land, this airy sweet is stabilized by gelatin. This hand-made version harkens back to childhood campfires and is completely suitable for S'mores.

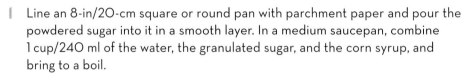

1 Line an 8-in/20-cm square or round pan with parchment paper and pour the powdered sugar into it in a smooth layer. In a medium saucepan, combine 1 cup/240 ml of the water, the granulated sugar, and the corn syrup, and bring to a boil.

2 Meanwhile, put the gelatin and the remaining ½ cup/120 ml water into the bowl of an electric mixer and let stand for 5 minutes. Then place the bowl onto the mixer fitted with the whisk attachment and mix on low speed.

3 The water-sugar mixture still on the stovetop should come to a rapid boil and cook until it reaches about 240°F/116°C. Once it does, slowly pour it into the gelatin mixture, and continue whipping on medium speed until light and fluffy, about 10 minutes. Add the vanilla and salt, then spread into the prepared pan. Let the marshmallow set until firm, for about 30 minutes at room temperature, then slice and dust with more powdered sugar.

Store in a zip-top plastic bag or an airtight container for 2 weeks at room temperature or 2 months in the freezer. (Marshmallow doesn't store well in the refrigerator.)

MAKES
about

1⅓
LB
(625 G)

TIME NEEDED
40 MIN

1 cup/100 g powdered sugar, sifted, plus more for dusting

1½ cups/360 ml water

2 cups/400 g granulated sugar

1 cup/240 ml corn syrup

2 tbsp gelatin

1 tbsp vanilla extract

1 tsp salt

Soft Chocolate Nougat

This familiar flavor contributes to many of our classic candy bars, like Over the Moon (page 30) and Chocolate Nougat Cups (page 45).

MAKES
about

4
CUPS
(795 G)

TIME NEEDED
20 MIN

3 cups/355 g ice

3 egg whites

¾ cup/150 g sugar

½ cup/120 ml corn syrup

¼ cup/60 ml water

½ cup/80 g melted high-quality dark chocolate

1 tbsp butter

1 tsp vanilla extract

½ tsp salt

1 Put the ice in a medium bowl and set aside. Line a baking sheet with parchment paper.

2 Put the egg whites in the bowl of an electric mixer fitted with a whisk attachment and set aside.

3 Stir together the sugar, corn syrup, and water in a medium saucepan. Bring to a boil over medium-high heat and continue to boil without stirring until the mixture reaches 225°F/110°C on a candy thermometer.

4 Begin whipping the egg whites on low speed. Continue cooking the sugar syrup until it reaches 245°F/118°C. (If your temperature goes higher, shock the syrup by setting the pan in the bowl of ice.) Pour a splash of the syrup into the egg whites, aiming for the space between the rim of the bowl and the whisk attachment. Continue whisking as you slowly add the rest of the hot sugar syrup. Increase the mixer speed to high and whip until the nougat reaches a full, frothy foam, about 2 minutes.

5 Allow the nougat to cool for about 20 minutes. (It should be close to room temperature and the bottom of the mixing bowl should no longer feel hot.) Turn the mixer on again and add the melted chocolate, butter, vanilla, and salt. Continue mixing until smooth. Use a big nonstick spatula or wooden spoon to scoop the nougat onto the prepared baking sheet. Allow the nougat to come to room temperature before using in candy-bar production.

Store in an airtight container at room temperature for 3 days or in the freezer for 2 months. (If frozen, thaw an hour in the refrigerator before using.)

Soft Vanilla Nougat

Nougat has a light, chewy consistency, a bright white color, and a charming ability to hold on to crunchy things like nuts or caramel pieces—as it does in our Nut 'n' Nougat Bars (page 44).

MAKES
about

4

CUPS
(785 G)

TIME NEEDED

20 MIN

3 cups/355 g ice

3 egg whites

1 cup/200 g sugar

½ cup/120 ml corn syrup

¼ cup/60 ml water

2 vanilla beans, scraped and seeded or 1 tbsp vanilla extract

½ tsp salt

1   Put the ice in a medium bowl and set aside.

2   Put the egg whites in the bowl of an electric mixer fitted with the whisk attachment and set aside.

3   Stir together the sugar, corn syrup, and water in a medium saucepan. Bring to a boil over medium heat and continue to boil without stirring until the mixture reaches 235°F/114°C on a candy thermometer, about 6 minutes.

4   Begin whipping the egg whites on low speed for about 1 minute, just until they are a little frothy. Continue cooking the sugar syrup until it reaches 245°F/118°C. (If your temperature goes higher, shock the syrup by setting the pan in the bowl of ice.) Pour a splash of the syrup into the egg whites, aiming for the space between the rim of the bowl and the whisk attachment. Continue whisking as you slowly add the rest of the hot sugar syrup. Increase the mixer speed to medium and whip until the nougat reaches a full, frothy foam, about 2 minutes.

5   Add the vanilla seeds and salt to the nougat. Keep whipping until it forms stiff peaks, about 3 minutes more. Allow to cool in the bowl. Once it is at room temperature, it's ready to use in candy-bar production.

Store in an airtight container at room temperature for 3 days or in the freezer for 2 months. (If frozen, thaw an hour in the refrigerator before using.)

Marzipan

This simple nut paste, with its classic combination of almonds and sugar, creates a very stable base for candy bars. When you make it from scratch, the almonds keep their subtle crunch, a plus for the artisan candy-crafter. We use it for our Caramel Pecan Tortoises (page 53), and in our Marzipan Flowers (variation, page 134) to decorate our dressed-up candy bars.

MAKES
about

1½
LB
(665 G)

TIME NEEDED
20 MIN

¾ cup/150 g granulated sugar

2 tbsp lemon juice

1 tbsp water

1 cup/115 g blanched raw almonds

2 egg whites

3 cups/300 g powdered sugar, sifted

1 tbsp vanilla extract

¼ tsp almond extract (optional)

1 tsp salt

In a small saucepan over medium heat, cook the granulated sugar, lemon juice, and water until it reaches 235°F/114°C on a candy thermometer. Meanwhile, process the almonds in a food processor until a paste forms, about 1 minute. When the sugar mixture is up to heat, pour it in through the feed tube of the food processor while the machine is in motion and blend until smooth. Add the egg whites and blend again until smooth. Pour the mixture into a large bowl and add the powdered sugar, vanilla, almond extract (if using), and salt. Stir with a spatula until the mixture is smooth. Break off pieces of the marzipan and shape as desired. (If desired, add food coloring to sculpt fruits or animals as in Caramel Pecan Tortoises, page 53.)

Store in a zip-top plastic bag in the refrigerator for 2 weeks or in the freezer for 6 months.

Yuletide Marzipan

Italians give marzipan, molded to look like fruit, as Christmas presents, and use it to decorate pastries during the holiday season.

Fondant

Fondant is one of the most important elements in building candy bars. A simple mix of sugar, water, and corn syrup, it changes dramatically as you heat it. The sugar crystals melt, then reform into a finer size as they cool. With some patience, this thick syrup becomes a sweet, semisolid paste that's perfect for such creations as our Chocolate & Nuts Inside & Out (page 29) or our Melty Chocolate Minties (page 50). While this basic recipe does not contain any cream, fondant's texture is mysteriously creamy and pleasing.

MAKES
about

2½
LB
(1.1 KG)

TIME NEEDED
about

50 MIN

3 cups/355 g ice

5 cups/1.2 kg sugar

1½ cups/360 ml water

⅓ cup/75 ml corn syrup

1 tbsp vanilla extract

1 tsp salt

1 Put the ice in a large bowl and set aside.

2 Combine the sugar and water in a large saucepan. Use a moist paper towel to wipe out any sugar that clings to the inside of the pan. Over medium heat, bring the mixture to a boil. Add the corn syrup and cook for 5 to 7 minutes. When the mixture reaches 238°F/115°C on a candy thermometer, pour it into the bowl of an electric mixer and allow to cool for about 1 minute. Place the bowl over the ice and let the syrup cool about 15 minutes more, to 110°F/42°C, before mixing.

3 Using the paddle attachment, mix the syrup on medium speed for at least 10 minutes. During this process, the syrup will change from a yellowish to a white, sticky liquid that eventually thickens into a paste. (See Fun With Fondant: Tips for Troubleshooting, Storing, and Using, page 108.) Once it does, add the vanilla and salt, remove the paste from the bowl, knead it a little with your hands, and it's ready to use.

Store in a zip-top plastic bag for 2 weeks in the refrigerator or for 3 months in the freezer.

Fun With Fondant

Fondant (page 106) has the most sublime consistency for candy making of all our candy components. Its ability to be firm, sweet, and meltingly soft all at once is what keeps candy makers loyal to it, despite its finicky nature.

Fondant starts as a boiled sugar syrup to which corn syrup is added. It must then be cooked to a very specific temperature (the middle range of the so-called soft-ball stage, 238°F/115°C), then cooled to a very specific temperature (110°F/42°C) on a marble slab or in a cold mixing bowl. Then, and only then, can it be stirred, and it must be stirred (or agitated as food scientists like to call it) for quite a long time. The sugar syrup changes into a solid, which is actually a mass of interlaced sugar crystals. The sugar crystals are coaxed into forming in a small size. Left untended or stirred too quickly, the crystals will form in a large size, which registers as a grainy texture on the palate. Grainy is frowned on in the confectionary business.

The first time you stir a handmade fondant, you will probably wonder, "Why is this taking so long?" And, "What am I doing wrong?" But fear not! It takes at least 10 minutes and often as much as 20 minutes of stirring a properly cooled fondant for it to set up with the coveted little crystals, so keep going. But because these crystals are so small, and it's hard to tell when you've achieved them, some graininess is common, especially when you're new to fondant making.

If things go badly and your fondant has a grainy texture, you might decide you can live with that. Go ahead and use the slightly imperfect fondant in your candy. If you prefer perfection, recook the grainy batch of fondant with 1 cup/240 ml of additional water and try, try again. The good news is that once you make a beautifully smooth batch of fondant, you can use it in many candy bars. It's very stable and can be refrigerated for 2 weeks or frozen for at least 3 months without losing its illusive and alluring texture.

Basic-Batch Caramel

Chocolate and caramel pair lusciously in many classic candy bars. This versatile caramel's texture is strong enough to structure a candy bar, yet soft enough to ooze out as you eat it. Its luxurious flavor affects everything around it. While some candy recipes suggest melting down commercial caramels as a time-saver, we strongly advise against it for flavor reasons. In bars like our Over the Moon (page 30) and Caramel Pecan Tortoises (page 53), we'll demonstrate the difference a batch of fresh caramel makes.

MAKES
about
1½
CUPS
(230 G)

TIME NEEDED
20 MIN

3 cups/355 g ice

1 cup/200 g sugar

¼ cup/60 ml water

2 tbsp corn syrup

½ cup/120 ml heavy cream

¼ cup/55 g butter

1 tbsp vanilla extract

½ tsp salt

1　Put the ice in a large bowl and set aside.

2　Combine the sugar and water in a medium saucepan. Stir the mixture until it resembles wet beach sand. Use a moist paper towel to wipe out any sugar that clings to the inside of the pan. (This keeps the crystals from getting into your syrup, which will make it gritty rather than smooth.) Over medium heat, bring the mixture to a boil without stirring. Add the corn syrup and cook for about 8 minutes, or until it first browns around the edges and then turns entirely the color of honey. When the mixture reaches about 310°F/154°C on a candy thermometer, carefully place the pan in the bowl of ice for a few seconds to stop the caramel from cooking.

3　Remove the caramel from the ice but let it cool for another 2 minutes, then add the cream, butter, vanilla, and salt, and stir with a wooden spoon. (Be careful! The still-hot syrup sizzles!) If some of the caramel has hardened on the bottom of the pan, return the pan to the stove and melt the bits into the mixture over low heat. Let the sauce cool a little more, then refrigerate for about 1 hour before using in candy-bar production.

Store in a covered bowl or an airtight container in the refrigerator for 1 week or in the freezer for 2 months.

Conquer Your Fear of Caramel

Caramel, bubbling furiously at high heat in an open pan, scares people. Yet the fact is that while most of us are comfortable turning an oven to 350°F/180°C, caramel cooks at a lower range: between 310 and 340°F/ 155 and 170°C. Given a few precautions on the part of the cook, caramel is actually wonderfully predictable, versatile, and safe to make.

Technically, when sugar and water boil together, the sugar crystals melt and bind with the water molecules to become a syrup, the syrup thickens, the water evaporates, and the remainder becomes the bittersweet amber concoction we know as caramel. In many of our candy-bar recipes, we rely on versions of this luscious sweet, so here are a few tips to help you past its sticky issues.

- Have a bowl of ice nearby. This serves two purposes: It provides an ice bath to help stop the caramel from cooking once it's done, and if you accidentally splash caramel on your skin, rubbing it with ice will sooth the burn.

- Wear latex gloves. Most pastry chefs don gloves to work with caramel. Look for the kind medical technicians wear, which are easy to find in drugstores. They're an extra layer of protection for your hands.

- Keep your movements to a minimum. No running around the kitchen with a pot of hot caramel! Have everything you need handy: ice bath, thermometer, nonstick spatula or wooden spoon, butter, cream, salt. Arrange these near the stovetop where you're cooking to minimize the risk of spills.

Dark-Chocolate Caramel

Some candy companies have responded to the recent uptick in dark chocolate's popularity by producing dark versions of old favorites. Dark chocolate's slight bitterness enhances caramel's salty sweetness. Two recipes that really play up this combination are our Chewy Caramel Bites (page 58) and our Dark Side of the Moon (see headnote, page 30).

MAKES
about

3
CUPS
(465 G)

TIME NEEDED
30 MIN

3 cups/355 g ice

2 cups/400 g sugar

¼ cup/60 ml water

¼ cup/60 ml corn syrup

½ cup/120 ml heavy cream

½ cup/115 g butter

1 tbsp vanilla extract

1 tsp salt

¾ cup/230 g high-quality dark chocolate (72 percent or bittersweet), finely chopped

1   Put the ice in a large bowl and set aside.

2   Combine the sugar and water in a medium saucepan. Stir the mixture until it resembles wet beach sand. Use a moist paper towel to wipe out any sugar that clings to the inside of the pan. Over medium heat, bring the mixture to a boil without stirring. Add the corn syrup and cook for about 8 minutes, or until it first browns around the edges and then turns entirely the color of honey. When the mixture reaches 310°F/154°C on a candy thermometer, carefully place the pan into the bowl of ice for a few seconds to stop the caramel from cooking.

3   Remove the caramel from the ice but let it cool for another 2 minutes, then add the cream, butter, vanilla, and salt, and stir with a wooden spoon. (Be careful! The still-hot syrup sizzles!) If some of the caramel has hardened on the bottom of the pan, return the pan to the stove and melt the bits into the mixture over low heat. Cool the sauce for 20 minutes, sprinkle in the chocolate, and stir until smooth. Cool to room temperature before using, or refrigerate for about 1 hour before using in candy-bar production.

Store in a covered bowl or an airtight container in the refrigerator for 1 week or in the freezer for 2 months.

Milk-Chocolate Caramel

MAKES
about

$4\frac{1}{2}$

CUPS
(520 G)

TIME NEEDED

30 MIN

3 cups/355 g ice

1½ cups/300 g sugar

½ cup/120 ml water

¼ cup/60 ml corn syrup

1 cup/240 ml heavy cream

6 tbsp/85 g butter

1 tsp vanilla extract

1 tsp salt

2 cups/310 g high-quality milk chocolate, finely chopped

Many candy-bar classics emphasize the love affair between milk chocolate and caramel. This recipe brings the two together as one—the perfect sexy marriage.

1 Put the ice in a large bowl and set aside.

2 Place the sugar and water in a medium saucepan. Stir the mixture until it resembles wet beach sand. Use a moist paper towel to wipe out any sugar that clings to the inside of the pan. Over medium heat, bring the mixture to a boil without stirring. Add the corn syrup and cook for about 8 minutes, or until it turns entirely golden brown, the color of honey. When the mixture reaches 310°F/154°C on a candy thermometer, carefully place the pan into the bowl of ice for a few seconds to stop the caramel from cooking.

3 Remove the caramel from the ice and let it cool for 2 minutes, then add the cream, butter, vanilla, and salt, and stir with a wooden spoon. (Be careful! The still-hot syrup sizzles!) If some of the caramel has hardened on the bottom of the pan, return the pan to the stove and melt the bits into the mixture over low heat. Cool the sauce for 20 minutes, sprinkle in the chocolate, and stir until smooth. For the firm, semisolid texture that's ideal for this caramel, refrigerate for 1 hour before using in candy-bar production.

Store in a covered bowl or an airtight container in the refrigerator for 1 week or in the freezer for 2 months.

Hard Caramel

In contrast to the softer caramels in our earlier recipes, most of the moisture in this one is cooked out, leaving a hard, super-crunchy, amber-colored candy in which nuts might be suspended, or that makes, on its own, dramatic, shard-like decorations for plated candy-bar desserts.

1 Put the ice in a large bowl and set aside. Line a baking sheet with parchment paper.

2 Combine the sugar and water in a medium saucepan. Stir the mixture until it resembles wet beach sand. Use a moist paper towel to wipe out any sugar that clings to the inside of the pan. Over medium heat, bring the mixture to a boil without stirring. Add the corn syrup and cook for about 8 minutes, or until it first browns around the edges and then turns entirely the color of honey. When the mixture reaches about 310°F/154°C on a candy thermometer, carefully place the pot in the bowl of ice to stop the caramel from cooking.

3 Carefully stir in the butter and salt. Pour the caramel over the prepared baking sheet and allow to set for 15 minutes. When hard, break up into pieces before using in candy-bar production.

Store in a zip-top plastic bag at room temperature for 3 to 4 days. (This does not keep well in the refrigerator or in the freezer.)

Variation: Nutty Caramel Add ¾ cup/90 g roasted nuts of your choice to the caramel at the end of the cooking process to create nut brittle, or just pour the caramel over the nuts on the prepared baking sheet.

Variation: Crushed Praline Powder Prepare the Nutty Caramel variation and allow the nut caramel to cool on the baking sheet, then put it in a food processor and pulse two or three times. This will create a crunchy praline powder that can be added to chocolate barks or nougat. Store the powder in an airtight container at room temperature for 2 to 3 days. (This will not stay crunchy if stored in the refrigerator or freezer.)

MAKES
about

1
CUP
(165 G)
CARAMEL
PIECES

TIME NEEDED
about

20 MIN

3 cups/355 g ice

1 cup/200 g sugar

½ cup/120 ml water

2 tbsp corn syrup

2 tbsp butter

1 tsp salt

Nutty Toffee

We cook our toffee more slowly than our hard caramel, and stir it a little so the butter won't scorch in the pan. A bit of baking soda adds lightness. Aficionados of butter-crunch bars (and we are two) will appreciate our Chocolate Butter-Toffee Snaps (page 52), a candy bar designed around the perfect ratio of airy crunch to smooth milk chocolate.

1 Put the ice in a large bowl and set aside. Line a baking sheet with parchment paper.

2 Combine the granulated sugar, brown sugar, butter, and water in a medium saucepan. Over medium heat, cook the mixture until it reaches 285°F/144°C on a candy thermometer. Set the pan in the bowl of ice to stop the caramel from cooking.

3 Allow the toffee to stop bubbling and add the vanilla and baking soda (which will make the mixture foam up). Mix thoroughly, add the nuts, and pour onto the prepared baking sheet. Cool for at least 20 minutes, then cut or break up into desired shapes before using in candy-bar production.

Store in a zip-top bag or an airtight container at room temperature for 3 to 4 days.

Variation: Mixed-Nut Toffee Add another 1/2 cup/60 g chopped roasted nuts (hazelnuts, peanuts, macadamias, walnuts, or pecans).

Variation: Not-So-Nutty Toffee Omit the nuts.

MAKES
about

2

**CUPS
(360 G)
TOFFEE
PIECES**

TIME NEEDED

30 MIN

3 cups/355 g ice

3/4 cup/150 g granulated sugar

3/4 cup/150 g brown sugar

1/2 cup/115 g butter

1/4 cup/60 ml water

1 tsp vanilla extract

1/4 tsp baking soda

1/2 cup/60 g almonds, preferably Marcona, chopped

No-Fail Chocolate Fudge

This fudge is easier to make than the Old-Fashioned Chocolate Fudge (facing page) because the sugar is stabilized in liquid form in the sweetened condensed milk. If you want quick, easy, delicious fudge, this is the one for you. Be sure to use high-quality chocolate for deep, dark chocolate flavor. Don't skimp on the best butter, such as Plugra or Kerrygold Irish. The richer taste really counts here.

1 Line an 8-in/20-cm square or round cake pan with parchment paper.

2 Place 2 cups/480 ml water in a medium pan over medium heat. Combine the chocolate and butter in a bowl that fits over the pan or in the top portion of a double boiler, and melt them together until smooth. Add the condensed milk and walnuts (if using) and stir with a wooden spoon until smooth. Pour the mixture into the prepared pan, smooth the top, cool to room temperature, cover with plastic wrap, and refrigerate for 1 to 2 hours before slicing.

Store in a zip-top plastic bag or wrapped tightly in plastic wrap for 1 week in the refrigerator or 2 months in the freezer.

MAKES
about
2
LB
(880 G)

TIME NEEDED
20 MIN
PLUS 1 TO 2 HOURS OF CHILLING IN THE REFRIGERATOR

3 cups/465 g finely chopped high-quality semisweet or bittersweet chocolate,

3 tbsp butter

One 14-oz/400-g can sweetened condensed milk

½ cup/55 g walnuts, roasted (see page 69; optional)

What Is Cream Candy?

What we often call cream candy, bonbons, or soft-centered candy can all be defined as crystalline sugar confections, explains chef Peter Greweling, a Certified Master Baker and professor at the Culinary Institute of America. The group includes fondant, fudge, maple candy, and pralines. Fondant is a system of minute sugar crystals surrounded by a saturated sugar solution; fudge is simply fondant with the addition of milkfat and flavoring. Maple candy is a crystallized version of maple syrup, and pralines are caramel relatives, sometimes with a fondant-like consistency.

Old-Fashioned Chocolate Fudge

MAKES
about

1¾
LB
(770 G)

TIME NEEDED

40 MIN

PLUS 1 TO 2 HOURS
OF CHILLING IN THE
REFRIGERATOR

2 cups/400 g sugar

¼ cup /60 ml corn syrup

⅓ cup/75 ml milk

¼ cup/60 ml heavy cream

2 tbsp butter

1 tbsp unsweetened cocoa powder

½ tsp salt

1 tsp vanilla extract

¾ cup/120 g finely chopped high-quality bittersweet chocolate

1½ cups/165 g walnuts, roasted (see page 69; optional)

In this recipe, you boil the sugar with corn syrup, fresh milk, heavy cream, and butter to create a syrup, then stir in premium dark chocolate. Be sure to let this mixture cool for at least 20 minutes (or to 110°F/42°C or below), then stir. This allows for a "fine-grain" fudge that is smooth, not gritty, on the palate.

1   Chill a large baking dish in the refrigerator. Line the bottom of an 8-in/20-cm square or round cake pan with parchment paper.

2   Combine the sugar, corn syrup, milk, and cream in a saucepan, then place over medium heat and bring to a boil. Allow the mixture to boil until it reaches 230°F/112°C on a candy thermometer, about 5 minutes. Remove from the heat and stir in the butter, cocoa powder, salt, vanilla, chocolate, and walnuts (if using). Return the pan to the heat and allow the mixture to boil until it reaches 238°F/115°C.

3   Remove the pan of hot fudge from the heat, pour into the chilled baking dish, and allow it to cool to 110°F/42°C. Stir the fudge with a wooden spoon until it thickens a little, then scoop it into the prepared cake pan. Cool to room temperature, cover with plastic wrap, and refrigerate for 1 to 2 hours before slicing.

Store in a zip-top plastic bag or wrapped tightly in plastic wrap for 1 week in the refrigerator or 2 months in the freezer.

Vanilla-Bean Fudge

Our white fudge is enriched with fresh vanilla bean, which adds black specs and an aromatic, subtle flavor. Whip some up for a Mix-and-Match bar when you want smooth, melting texture with extra vanilla.

MAKES
about

1½
LB
(680 G)

TIME NEEDED

30 MIN
PLUS 1 TO 2 HOURS
OF CHILLING IN THE
REFRIGERATOR

3 cups/600 g sugar

½ cup/120 ml corn syrup

1 cup/240 ml heavy cream

1 tsp vanilla extract

1 vanilla bean, scraped and seeded

¾ cup/90 g chopped pecans, lightly roasted (see page 69; optional)

½ tsp salt

1 Chill a large baking dish in the refrigerator. Line the bottom of an 8-in/20-cm square or round cake pan with parchment paper.

2 In a medium saucepan, combine the sugar, corn syrup, and cream and stir until sugar is dissolved. Cook over medium heat until a candy thermometer inserted into the mixture reads 238°F/115°C. Remove from the heat, and pour into the chilled baking dish. Allow to cool to 110°F/42°C, about 15 minutes. Stir in the vanilla extract and vanilla seeds. Continue stirring until the fudge starts to thicken. Stir in the pecans and salt. Pour the fudge into the prepared pan, allow it to cool to room temperature, then refrigerate covered for 1 to 2 hours before slicing.

Store in a zip-top plastic bag or wrapped tightly in plastic for 1 week in the refrigerator or for 2 months in the freezer.

Variation: Maple Fudge Add 2 tbsp pure maple syrup when you add the vanilla.

Variation: Milk-Chocolate Fudge Add ¾ cup/115 g chopped milk chocolate when you add the vanilla.

Milk-Chocolate Ganache

Chocolate and cream mixed together make a classic sauce known as *ganache*, which means "fool" in French. Legend has it that when a certain clumsy cook spilled hot cream into a bowl of chocolate, his boss called him a ganache. But foolishness can lead to greatness—in this case, to a versatile sauce that makes a fine cake icing or candy-bar filling and that is used in pastry kitchens around the world.

MAKES
about

3½
CUPS
(535 G)

TIME NEEDED
about

20 MIN

1 cup/155 g finely chopped high-quality milk chocolate

¾ cup/180 ml heavy cream

1 tsp vanilla extract

½ tsp salt

1 Put 2 cups/480ml water in a medium saucepan and bring to a boil.

2 Place the milk chocolate in a medium stainless-steel or Pyrex bowl or in the top portion of a double boiler. Place the bowl over the boiling water and turn off the heat.

3 Put the cream, vanilla, and salt into a small saucepan and bring to a simmer.

4 Remove the bowl of chocolate from the hot water when the chocolate is softened. (You don't have to melt it all the way.) Pour the simmering cream mixture over the chocolate in the bowl. Allow it to sit for about 30 seconds, then stir. This mixture looks very lumpy at first but as you continue stirring, it smooths out into a shiny sauce. Once it does, refrigerate for 20 to 30 minutes, until it is firm enough to spread.

Store in an airtight container for 1 week in the refrigerator or for 2 months in the freezer.

Variation: Dark-Chocolate or White-Chocolate Ganache Swap in either dark chocolate or white chocolate for the milk chocolate.

Variation: Hazelnut-Chocolate Ganache Add 2 tbsp hazelnut butter (also known as praline paste, see Shopping Resources Guide, page 150) and 2 tbsp broken, roasted hazelnuts after the ganache is smooth.

Variation: Light Chocolate Ganache Replace the cream in the ganache with 2 percent milk.

Strawberry Jam

The vibrant freshness of homemade strawberry jam and its faint crunch of strawberry seeds makes us wonder why we even bother to buy it in a jar.

Place the strawberries, sugar, lemon juice, and salt in a saucepan and boil over medium heat for 10 to 12 minutes, stirring occasionally. Pour the jam into a 2-cup/480-ml measuring cup and allow it to cool at room temperature for about 10 minutes. Refrigerate it for 20 minutes to fully set before using in candy-bar production.

Store, covered, in the refrigerator for 2 weeks.

MAKES
about

1½

CUPS
(345 G)

TIME NEEDED

40 MIN

2 cups/305 g hulled strawberries

½ cup/100 g sugar

1 tbsp lemon juice

½ tsp salt

Chocolate Sugar Cookies

Offering a little chocolate, a little crunch, and a sturdy platform for some of our Mix-and-Match bars, these cookies (pictured on page 122, left) also crumble up nicely for our White-Chocolate Cookies & Crunch Bars (page 36).

MAKES
about

40
COOKIES

TIME NEEDED
about

1HR

1½ cups/185 g cake flour, sifted

¾ cup/70 g unsweetened cocoa powder, sifted

1 tsp salt

¾ cup/170 g cold unsalted butter

1½ cups/300 g sugar

1 egg

1 tbsp rum

1 tbsp brewed espresso or coffee

1 tsp vanilla extract

1 Preheat the oven to 350°F/180°C/gas 4. Sift together the cake flour, cocoa powder, and salt in a medium bowl, stir with a whisk, and set aside.

2 In the bowl of an electric mixer fitted with the paddle attachment, cream the butter at low speed for about 2 minutes, until it is soft and fluffy. Slowly beat in the sugar, add the egg, and mix on low. Turn off the mixer and slowly add half of the dry ingredients. Resume mixing on low until they're incorporated. Add the remaining dry ingredients, then the rum, espresso, and vanilla and mix until smooth.

3 Remove the dough from the mixer and form it into a disc. Cover with plastic wrap or put in a zip-top plastic bag and chill for about 30 minutes. Shape the dough as needed for a candy-bar recipe: Roll into 3-in-/7.5-cm-long logs and leave whole or cut into small, round discs (about 2 in/5 cm in diameter). Bake until the edges darken slightly and the center is set, 12 to 15 minutes. Allow to cool before using in candy-bar production.

Store in a zip-top plastic bag at room temperature for 2 days or in the freezer for 2 months. (These lose their crispness if stored in the refrigerator.)

Very-Vanilla Sugar Cookies

MAKES
about

40

COOKIES

TIME NEEDED

30 MIN

2 cups/255 g all-purpose flour, sifted

1 tsp salt

1 cup/225 g cold unsalted butter

1 vanilla bean, scraped and seeded

¾ cup/150 g sugar

1 extra-large egg, plus 1 egg yolk

3 tbsp heavy cream

1 tbsp vanilla extract

This recipe (pictured opposite, right) is based on the sweet French pastry dough known as *pâte sucrée*. Richly flavored and tender, it's often used as a tart crust because of its sturdiness. Its buttery crunch makes it an ideal support for the chocolate and caramel in bars like our Cocoa-Nib Caramel Cookie Sticks (page 34). One more plus: The cookies don't spread when you bake them, so you can create the exact shape you want for your candy bar.

1 Preheat the oven to 350°F/180°C/gas 4. Sift together the flour and salt in a medium bowl and set aside.

2 In the bowl of an electric mixer fitted with the paddle attachment, cream the butter and vanilla seeds together just until the butter softens. Add the sugar and mix until lightly fluffy, just under 1 minute. Add the whole egg, egg yolk, cream, and vanilla extract and mix until they're incorporated. Stop the mixer and add half of the flour-salt mixture, then mix on low until smooth. Add the remaining flour-salt mixture and mix on low until the dough comes together. Place the dough on a parchment-lined work surface or large cutting board. Shape it into a flat disc, wrap it in plastic wrap, and chill in the refrigerator for 30 minutes until firm.

3 Roll out the dough on a lightly floured work surface and shape according to your recipe (i.e., 3-in/7.5-cm logs for Cocoa-Nib Caramel Cookie Sticks, or 1-in/2.5-cm discs for Hazelnut Strawberry Jams). Bake for 12 to 15 minutes, until the edges are light brown and the center is set. (If the cookies are flat discs, they will bake a little faster than logs. Keep an eye on them!) Allow to cool before using in candy-bar production.

Store in a zip-top plastic bag at room temperature for 2 days or in the freezer for 2 months. (These will lose their crispness if stored in the refrigerator.)

Brown Sugar–Crisps

Thin to win! This recipe packs light crunch and deep brown-sugar richness into a snappy wafer. Roll the cookie dough out thin (1/8 in/4 mm) with a rolling pin, bake, and use in candy-bar sandwiches (like our Crispy Cookie Crunch, page 33). Or just dip the cookies straight into melted chocolate.

MAKES
about
60
COOKIES

TIME NEEDED
50MIN

1 cup/200 g firmly packed light brown sugar

1/2 cup/115 g butter

3 tbsp molasses

2 cups/250 g all-purpose flour, sifted

2 tbsp unsweetened cocoa powder

1/2 tsp baking soda

1/2 tsp salt

1 tbsp vanilla extract

1   Preheat the oven to 350°F/180°C/gas 4. Line a baking sheet with parchment paper.

2   Cook the brown sugar, butter, and molasses together in a medium saucepan over medium heat until the butter has melted and the mixture bubbles, about 3 minutes.

3   Meanwhile, in a large bowl, sift together the flour, cocoa powder, baking soda, and salt. Stir the hot butter mixture into the dry ingredients. Add the vanilla, and stir until smooth. The mixture will become a dark dough. Put the dough in an extra-large, zip-top plastic bag and chill in the refrigerator for at least 30 minutes.

4   With a floured rolling pin, roll out the dough 1/8 in/4 mm thick. Use a cookie cutter to cut out 11/2-in/4-cm discs (or any desired shape, such as squares, triangles, or hearts). Put the discs on the prepared baking sheet and bake for about 10 minutes, until the edges are crispy. Cool completely before using in candy-bar production.

Store in an airtight container or a zip-top plastic bag for 3 days at room temperature or 2 months in the freezer. (These lose their crunch if stored in the refrigerator.)

Candy Cookies

The word *cookie* comes from the Dutch word *koekje*, which means "little cake." Cookies are indeed derived from baked batters, just like cakes. But they have become a confectionary category all their own, complete with eight official classifications based on how they're made or shaped: bagged, dropped, rolled, molded, refrigerator, bar, sheet, and stencil. The cookies most useful to the candy-bar maker are the rolled variety, such as our Brown Sugar–Crisps, which allow for careful shaping and delicate crunch, and molded types like the Very-Vanilla Sugar Cookie (page 123), which can hold a firm shape under several gooey layers.

Tempered Dark Chocolate

Choose high-quality dark chocolate with a cocoa content of 60 percent or higher. The higher the percentage, the darker the appearance and the stronger the chocolate's taste will be.

MAKES

2⅔
CUPS
(800 G)

TIME NEEDED

20 MIN

3 cups/355 g ice

3 cups/465 g chopped high-quality dark chocolate

1 Put the ice in a large bowl and set aside.

2 Reserve a handful of the chopped chocolate, and melt the rest gently in a stainless-steel bowl set over simmering water until it reaches 115°F/45°C on a candy thermometer. Remove the bowl from the heat. Wipe the bottom of the bowl with a dry cloth to prevent water from splashing onto the work surface.

3 Sprinkle the reserved chocolate into the melted chocolate and stir. Cool the chocolate by placing over the bowl of ice for a few seconds at a time, removing it, stirring until smooth, and repeating until the temperature drops to 82°F/31°C.

4 Heat the chocolate again by placing the chocolate bowl back over the simmering water for 30 seconds to 1 minute at a time. Once its temperature rises to 90°F/34°C, the chocolate is ready to use in candy-bar production.

Keep Your Temper!

It's important to keep tempered chocolate at 90°F/34°C. But as we begin to dip our candy bars in a bowl of tempered chocolate, the chocolate cools. When this happens, set the bowl of chocolate over a pan of hot water for about 30 seconds at a time, until it returns to the 90°F/34°C mark. And be careful not to overheat your chocolate because all the stable crystals will melt and you will have to start over. It shouldn't rise above 91°F/35°C!

Tempered Milk Chocolate

Milk chocolate's flavor, while less powerful than that of dark chocolate, is just as precious. Choose a premium brand with 38 to 50 percent cacao.

MAKES

2⅔
CUPS
(800 G)

TIME NEEDED

20 MIN

3 cups/355 g ice

3 cups/465 g chopped high-quality milk chocolate

1 Put the ice in a large bowl and set aside.

2 Reserve a handful of the chopped chocolate, and melt the rest gently in a stainless-steel bowl set over simmering water until it reaches 115°F/45°C on a candy thermometer. Remove the bowl from the heat. Wipe the bottom of the bowl with a dry cloth to prevent water from splashing onto the work surface.

3 Sprinkle the reserved chocolate into the melted chocolate and stir. Cool the chocolate by placing over the bowl of ice for a few seconds at a time, removing it, stirring until smooth, and repeating until the temperature drops to 82°F/31°C.

4 Heat the chocolate again by placing the chocolate bowl back over the simmering water for 30 seconds to 1 minute at a time. Once its temperature rises to 89°F/34°C, the chocolate is ready to use in candy-bar production.

Tempering: Too Much Trouble?

Many of our bars rely on tempered chocolate for their glossy surface and firm texture. Tempering chocolate is time-consuming and sometimes daunting (see Keep Your Temper!, page 127). Why do it? *Untempered* chocolate stays softer. It might develop a blemished surface caused by fat bloom (when cocoa-butter crystals align with each other instead of staying integrated with the cocoa solids), which is visually unappealing but not nutritionally dangerous. Bloom won't appear if you keep candy bars refrigerated until serving. If you don't really care about a perfect, shiny surface, just dip the bars in melted dark or milk chocolate, shake them off, and refrigerate until serving time.

Tempered White Chocolate

White chocolate is white for a reason: Its simple formula lacks cocoa solids altogether. Nevertheless, as with tempered dark and milk chocolate, using a high-quality version of white will result in a better candy bar. See Keep Your Temper!, page 127, for tips on temperature.

MAKES

2⅔

**CUPS
(800 G)**

TIME NEEDED

20 MIN

3 cups/355 g ice

3 cups/465 g chopped high-quality white chocolate

1   Put the ice in a large bowl and set aside.

2   Reserve a handful of the chopped chocolate, and melt the rest gently in a stainless-steel bowl set over simmering water until it reaches 115°F/45°C on a candy thermometer. Remove the bowl from the heat. Wipe the bottom of the bowl with a dry cloth to prevent water from splashing onto the work surface.

3   Sprinkle the reserved chocolate into the melted chocolate and stir. Cool the chocolate by placing over the bowl of ice for a few seconds at a time, removing it, stirring until smooth, and repeating until the temperature drops to 82°F/31°C.

4   Heat the chocolate again by placing the chocolate bowl back over the simmering water for 30 seconds to 1 minute. Once its temperature rises to 88°F/33°C, the chocolate is ready to use in candy-bar production.

CHAPTER 6
GILDING THE LILY

Dressing Bars for Dessert

The bars you'll make with this book are all company fare, delicious enough for discerning palates. But if you're going to serve them for dessert, think about crowning your creations with a chocolate rose or marzipan lily or a drizzle of warm, salty caramel sauce. In this chapter, we'll give you recipes for turning your bars into art as well as tips on designing candy-bar dessert platters and plates.

The guidelines chefs use to make artistic, eye-catching presentations (a practice known as plating) are these: The plate should be carefully composed with vibrant and/or contrasting colors; the textures on the plate should vary; height should be created by using tall cookies or skewered fruit; and the plate design should include negative space. A main item (in our case, candy bars) should be adorned by sauces and garnishes in a dramatic design. The decorations and sauces in this section are designed to highlight the colors and textures of artisan candy bars on plates, platters, and festive tables.

Dark-Chocolate Flowers

Handmade flowers allow you to create a sophisticated look for your candy bars, one that matches all the hard work and love you put into them. This recipe forms a thick, versatile chocolate paste known as chocolate plastique. As you see in the photo, you can easily make rose petals to grace the tops of candy bars and dessert plates.

MAKES
about

40
FLOWERS

TIME NEEDED
about

1HR **30**MIN

1 batch **Chocolate Taffy (page 61)**

1   Line a baking sheet with parchment paper.

2   Using a rolling pin, roll out a disc of taffy on a piece of parchment to about ¼ in/6 mm thick. Cut small circles in the taffy using the back of a pastry-bag tip. If you don't have a pastry-bag tip, use a bottle top from a milk jug or anything that cuts uniform circles about 1 in/2.5 cm in diameter.

3   Separate the circles (which we will now call petals) on the parchment paper and flatten the outer edges of each petal with the back of a spoon to make them almost transparent. Peel the first petal off the parchment (a small spatula helps with this job) and roll it tight, like a cigar. Pick up the next petal and wrap it around the first one, pinching the two together at the base. Each petal should get successively looser and wider, mimicking the way a rose bloom opens. Place each completed rose on the prepared baking sheet. Cover the baking sheet with plastic wrap and refrigerate until ready to use.

Store in a zip-top plastic bag or tightly wrapped in plastic in the refrigerator for 2 weeks or in the freezer for 6 months.

CONTINUED

Variation: White-Chocolate Flowers Use white chocolate instead of dark when you make the Chocolate Taffy and reduce the amount of corn syrup to ½ cup/120 ml.

Variation: Marzipan Flowers Use 1 batch Marzipan (page 104), cooled to room temperature, or ¾ cup/170 g store-bought marzipan.

Fondant Roses

One method cake decorators use to make decorative roses involves hand-shaping colored rolled fondant, which is similar to the fondant centers of our candy bars but less sticky and easier to work with. Available from bakery supply shops, it's specifically designed for decorating cakes, but it works well on candy bars, too. Tint it with food coloring, sparingly applied, so colors look natural. (Novice decorators often overuse coloring and wind up with neon-hued roses—fun, but not particularly elegant or appetizing.)

When you have the shade you want, follow the instructions for making Dark-Chocolate Flowers and adorn your candy bars with them.

Candied Mint Leaves

These are great to have on hand whenever you need to spice up a candy-bar creation with a bit of minty crunch. They're easy to make but require 1 hour to dry out thoroughly in a very low oven.

1 Line a baking sheet with parchment paper. Place the sugar in a shallow bowl.

2 Dip the mint leaves into a pan of room-temperature tap water just long enough to soften, about 5 seconds. Scoop them out with a strainer, then dip them one at a time in the sugar to coat heavily on both sides. Put the leaves on the prepared baking sheet, and bake 1 hour in a low oven (100 to 200°F/38 to 95°C).

Store in an airtight container at room temperature for 2 weeks. (In humid conditions, the leaves may lose their vibrant color, so they are best used within a week or two.)

MAKES
about

1
CUP
(95 G)

TIME NEEDED
about

1 HR **30** MIN

1 cup/200 g sugar

¾ cup/20 g fresh mint leaves

Candied Citrus

Candied citrus zest and slices, which we use in our barks and as decoration, conjure an old-fashioned delight. Before fruit chews were sold at every gas station, grocery store, and movie theatre, people enjoyed this simple confection of sugary fruit zest and slices dried to a chewy finish. When we zest our citrus (shave off the orange part of the orange peel, or the yellow part of the lemon peel), we avoid the white underside, or pith, because it's bitter. We dip first in boiling water, then in simple syrup to sweeten away any hint of bitterness.

MAKES

2

CUPS
(300 G)

TIME NEEDED
about

1 HR 20 MIN

3 lemons

3 oranges

3 limes

1 batch Simple Syrup (page 139), cooled

Coarse or granulated sugar for dusting

1   Line a baking sheet or 8-in/20-cm cake pan with parchment paper.

2   Bring two medium saucepans of water to a boil over medium-high heat. Zest 2 lemons, 2 oranges, and 2 limes with a zester or small paring knife, separating the colored skin from the white pith. Cut each piece of zest into thin strips and transfer to a medium strainer or small colander. Dip the strips into the first pan of boiling water for about 20 seconds, then the second pan of boiling water for about 20 seconds, and transfer them to the pan of simple syrup.

3   Cut the remaining lemon, orange, and lime into thin slices. Dip them into the first pan of boiling water for about 20 seconds, then the second pan for 20 seconds, then put them in the pan of simple syrup.

CONTINUED

4   Drain all the zest and fruit slices on a paper towel, pat dry, and shower generously with coarse sugar (also known as crystal sugar) before placing on the prepared baking sheet. Allow them to dry out in a 100 to 200°F/38 to 95°C oven for about 1 hour or, if possible, in an unheated oven overnight.

Store in an airtight container at room temperature for 2 weeks. (In humid conditions, candied citrus may lose its vibrant color, so it is best used within a week or two.)

Variation: Candied Grapefruit Substitute grapefruit for the other citrus fruits.

Simple Syrup

A basic sugar-and-water solution that can do everything from sweetening cocktails to moistening cakes, simple syrup comes in handy when we make candied citrus zest. The peel soaks up the syrup's sweetness while its slight stickiness encourages the granulated sugar to adhere before the peel dries.

Place sugar, water, vanilla, and salt in a medium saucepan and boil over medium heat. Once the syrup has boiled, turn off the heat, cool for about 20 minutes, and it's ready to use.

Store in an airtight container in the refrigerator for 3 weeks.

MAKES
about
1
CUP
(240 ML)

TIME NEEDED
20 MIN

¾ cup/150 g sugar

¾ cup/180 ml water

1 tsp vanilla extract

½ tsp salt

Easy Vanilla Butter-cream

MAKES
about

4

CUPS
(920 G)

TIME NEEDED

30 MIN

2 cups/455 g butter

¹/₂ cup/115 g shortening

3 cups/300 g powdered sugar, sifted, plus more if needed

¹/₂ cup/120 ml water, plus more if needed

1 tbsp vanilla extract

¹/₂ tsp salt

Food coloring (optional)

If you're at all artistically inclined, we encourage you to make buttercream, color it, and try piping some fetching flowers with a pastry bag onto your handmade candy bars. This type of buttercream is prized by cake decorators because of its stability—it doesn't melt as easily as other types—and its reliable consistency for piping.

1 In the bowl of an electric mixer fitted with the paddle attachment, cream the butter on low speed until it's soft and fluffy, about 2 minutes. Add the shortening and mix to combine. Stop the mixer and add half of the powdered sugar, mix on low until smooth, then stop and add the remaining powdered sugar. Add the water, vanilla, and salt, then switch to the whisk attachment and mix on medium speed for 2 minutes. If the buttercream is too soft, add a little more sifted powdered sugar, or refrigerate for 20 minutes, then rewhip. If it's too firm, add a little more water. Mix in the food coloring (if using).

2 Transfer the buttercream to a piping bag fitted with a pastry tip, or transfer to a zip-top plastic bag for storage.

Store in the refrigerator for 1 week or in the freezer for 2 months.

Easy Chocolate Butter-cream

MAKES
about

4
CUPS
(920 G)

TIME NEEDED
about

30 MIN

2¾ cups/270 g powdered sugar, plus more if needed

¼ cup/20 g unsweetened cocoa powder

2 cups/455 g butter

½ cup/115 g shortening

½ cup/120 ml water, plus more if needed

1 tbsp vanilla extract

½ tsp salt

For those of you who (like us) can never get enough chocolate, this one's for you.

1   Sift the powdered sugar and cocoa powder onto a piece of parchment paper and set aside.

2   In the bowl of an electric mixer fitted with the paddle attachment, cream the butter on low speed until it's soft and fluffy, about 2 minutes. Add the shortening and mix to combine. Stop the mixer and add half of the powdered sugar and cocoa powder, mix on low until smooth, then stop and add the remaining sugar-cocoa mixture. Add the water, vanilla, and salt, then switch to the whisk attachment, and mix on medium speed for 2 minutes. If the buttercream is too soft, add a little more sifted powdered sugar, or refrigerate for 20 minutes, then rewhip. If it's too firm, add a little more water.

3   Transfer the buttercream to a piping bag fitted with a pastry tip, or transfer to a zip-top plastic bag for storage.

Store in the refrigerator for 1 week, or in the freezer for 2 months.

Tips on Tips

Pastry tips are an obsession for cake decorators and a slightly intimidating bit of hardware for the uninitiated. While some tips can create elaborate shapes that mimic the intricacies of flower petals, the artisan candy maker really only needs a few basics. Each different tip has a number etched on its side to indicate its size. The plain-edged ones are round tips, and the more decorative, fluted ones are star tips. For jobs like piping nougat onto cookies, candy makers use sturdy, medium-size tips such as the Ateco 804 round tip or the 843 star tip. To decorate fancy candy bars, smaller, more intricate tips come in handy.

Caramel Sauce

This light caramel sauce creates elegant pools for candy bars served as plated desserts.

MAKES
about
2
CUPS
(505 G)

TIME NEEDED
20 MIN

3 cups/355 g ice

1 cup/200 g sugar

¼ cup/60 ml water

¼ cup/60 ml corn syrup

1 cup/240 ml cream

¼ cup/55 g butter

1 tbsp vanilla extract

1 tsp salt

1 Put the ice in a large bowl and set aside.

2 Combine the sugar, water, and corn syrup in a medium saucepan. Stir the mixture until it resembles wet beach sand. Use a moist paper towel to wipe out any sugar that clings to the inside of the pan. (This keeps the crystals from getting into your syrup, which will make it gritty rather than smooth.) Over medium heat, bring the mixture to a boil without stirring. Cook for about 8 minutes, or until the mixture reaches 290°F/146°C on a candy thermometer and first browns around the edges, then turns entirely golden brown.

3 Meanwhile, heat the cream in a separate small saucepan. When the boiling sugar reaches 290°F/146°C, remove from the heat and place pan in the bowl of ice for about 30 seconds to stop the caramel from cooking.

4 Stir in the hot cream, then the butter. (Careful! This will bubble up!) Add the vanilla and salt. Cool the caramel for about 15 minutes, then transfer it to a small bowl. Using a big soupspoon, decorate a plate or platter as desired with the sauce, allow it to cool completely, and arrange candy-bar pieces atop your designs to serve.

Store covered in a small bowl in the refrigerator for 1 week or in the freezer for 2 months. (Must be rewarmed over a water bath before using again.)

Orange-Brandy Caramel Sauce

This orange-brandy-sugar combination has inspired many students at Le Cordon Bleu College of Culinary Arts, where Susie teaches. It distinguishes the über-desserts Crêpes Suzette and Bananas Foster. We drench cookies in this sauce for our Orange-Chocolate Cookie Crunch Bars (page 83), and it also makes a flavorful sauce to use for plated desserts.

MAKES
about
1½
CUPS
(320 G)

TIME NEEDED
20 MIN

3 cups/355 g ice

1 cup/200 g sugar

¼ cup/60 ml water

2 tbsp corn syrup

½ cup/120 ml orange juice

Zest from 1 orange

¼ cup/60 ml Grand Marnier

1 tbsp lemon juice

½ cup/120 ml cream, slightly warmed

½ cup/110 g butter

1 tsp vanilla extract

1 tsp salt

1   Put the ice in a large bowl and set aside.

2   Combine the sugar, water, corn syrup, orange juice and zest, Grand Marnier, and lemon juice in a medium saucepan. Stir the mixture until it resembles wet beach sand. Use a moist paper towel to wipe out any sugar that clings to the inside of the pan. Over medium heat, bring the mixture to a boil without stirring. Cook for about 8 minutes, or until the mixture reaches 290°F/146°C on a candy thermometer and begins to turn brown at the edges. Keep cooking until the entire batch turns a medium brown, the color of honey. This is about 310°F/154°C on the thermometer. Place the pan in the bowl of ice to stop the caramel from cooking.

3   Remove the pan from the ice but let the caramel cool for several more minutes. Add the cream, butter, vanilla, and salt. (Be careful! It sizzles!) Allow this mixture to cool about 20 minutes more before using in candy-bar production or as a sauce.

Store at room temperature for 24 hours, or in a wrapped bowl in the refrigerator for 2 weeks. (Must be rewarmed over a water bath before using again.)

Raspberry Sauce

The most beautiful red in the pastry chef's repertoire comes from melted raspberries. This sauce adds vibrant color and contrast to dessert plates, in addition to fresh raspberry flavor. Raspberry Sauce complements any of our sliced candy-bar creations, and it also goes very well with our Vanilla-Bean Sauce (facing page) or a citrus sauce such as our Orange-Brandy Caramel Sauce (page 143). You can continue contrasting and heightening the color on your plates by garnishing them with fresh mint leaves, raspberries, and pomegranate seeds.

Put raspberries, sugar, vanilla, brandy, and salt in a medium saucepan over medium heat. Stir until the raspberries melt and the juices thicken, 8 to 10 minutes. Strain the sauce into a small bowl or squeeze bottle and use as desired.

Store in a squeeze bottle or covered plastic storage cup in the refrigerator for 3 to 4 days or in the freezer for 2 months. Rewarm to use.

MAKES
about
3/4
CUP
(155 G)

TIME NEEDED
20 MIN

2 cups/345 g fresh or frozen raspberries

2 tbsp sugar

1 tsp vanilla extract

1 tsp brandy

1/2 tsp salt

Vanilla-Bean Sauce

The well-known vanilla sauce, *crème anglaise*, is often described as the mother sauce of the bakeshop because of its versatility: Once you make it, you can flavor it with chocolate, coffee, Kahlua, brandy—and the list goes on. Our version is delicately speckled with vanilla seeds and goes with fruit desserts, chocolate desserts, and, of course, candy bars.

MAKES
about

1

CUP
(200 G)

TIME NEEDED

30 MIN

1 vanilla bean, scraped and seeded

½ cup/120 ml milk

½ cup/120 ml cream

2 eggs

½ cup/100 g sugar

1 Combine the vanilla-bean seeds and pod, milk, and cream in a medium saucepan and bring to a simmer. Meanwhile, whisk the eggs and sugar together in a medium bowl. When the milk mixture scalds, pour about a quarter of it into the egg mixture and continue whisking. Pour in one quarter more and continue whisking, repeating until all the hot milk mixture is incorporated. Remove the vanilla-bean pod, rinse it off, and reserve for later use.

2 Rinse the saucepan, return it to the stovetop, and pour the sauce into it over medium heat. Allow the sauce to heat to 180°F/82°C on a candy thermometer while you stir, about 5 minutes. Pour the sauce through a sieve into a small bowl or squeeze bottle and use as desired.

While the sauce is best used fresh, it can be stored in the refrigerator for 3 days or in the freezer for 2 weeks. Rewarm to use.

Candy Bar Platters and Plates

We're all used to candy bars as easy, on-the-go snacks. So when you serve them as desserts to guests, we have a few tips on presentation. Of course, this is up to you, and we've found that few people we know will turn down a platter piled with chocolate, even unadorned, on a plate. But a bit of ceremony does honor your labor of love, and prepares your lucky guests to receive it.

Since candy bars are inherently informal—all those childhood associations—you've got lots of choice in how you show them off. Still, there are general guidelines that make most food more appealing when you serve it. Ideally, it's somewhat colorful on the plate, with interesting contrasts of texture and tone. It doesn't fight with that plate, which is mostly background for the main event. Garnish is secondary but important; it should hint at the food's flavors and not just complicate its look.

So lay out your bars, if you offer a sampling, to show their differences—the neat, round cups; the sliced squares with gooey, layered innards; the long, thin cookie sticks. A white platter is a good choice for a mix since it frames candy simply and highlights details like caramel drizzles and chocolate flowers without looking cluttered. Depending on the bars it holds, you can dust it with cocoa or edge it with chocolate curls, shaved from a block with a vegetable grater. Or tuck fresh mint sprigs beside the Melty Chocolate Minties, fresh strawberries beside your PB & J Supreme Discs. Citrus zest, whole roasted nuts, or coconut shavings make sweet touches too against the white, and add appetizing fragrances.

But having said all that, we hope you'll please yourself and go with your eye (and nose and heart) in presenting your bars. We've done this many ways ourselves and seen how chocolate pops on turquoise plates—or Christmas-red or summer-orange—and how it sings on a green milk-glass tray. Even a complicated, rose-patterned platter did us proud once (though we opted for a single bar type instead of several, there), as did a stark black one lined with a crisp white parchment square. We have laid Chocolate Nougat Cups in pools of raspberry sauce in soup plates and dripped chocolate dots around the edges. We've sprinkled powdered sugar on Chocolate Taffy and cocoa nibs on Chocolate-Dipped Strawberries, arranging both on cake stands laid with buttercream lilies. We have piped borders on our Coconut Clouds and ruffles on our Crispy Cookie Crunch. But we have also handed plain bars around on napkins. And no one has ever complained.

Wrapping Them Up

CANDY BAR GIFTS TO GO

By now, over these last few chapters, you will have crafted some gorgeous sweets—shockingly delicious and lovely to look at. Many of these might not have made it past your door, given everyone who suddenly appears once the kitchen fills with the smells of baking cookies, caramel, and warm milk chocolate. But sooner or later, those of us who fall hard for candy making realize what a gift our creations make for others. Having put so much into crafting them, we must think up wrappings that do them justice, because really, they're so beautiful, who can just stick them in any old box?

Commercial candy companies can't afford the time or resources to dress bars in special wraps and ribbons, but we can. It's part of the fun, dreaming up the right package for what we've got—even one never intended for a hand-made candy bar. On the hunt for unique trimmings, the two of us have wound up in unlikely spots—hardware stores, bath shops, Japan- and Chinatowns, not to mention all manner of flea markets, odd-lot discounters, kitchen supply stores, and paperies. We have signed up to access treasure troves of great packaging at wholesale container websites and gone on tears through mark-down merchandisers. What have we found? Little boxes of all kinds: bamboo, inlaid-wood, papier-mâché, glass with snap-on tops, lacquered, beaded, painted, quilted, jeweled. Soap dishes—modern, vintage, china, pottery. Quirky coin purses! Beautiful take-out food containers! Faux-fur bags! Fabric remnants! Handmade paper! Amazingly patterned padded mailers!

The more you're on the lookout for things to tuck candy bars in, the more you'll find. Some packages will be throw-aways, some keepers, once the bars are gone. All are part of the gift, and the (maybe a little over-the-top) thought you lavish on it.

Even before you reach the wrapping stage, we recommend gathering some pals for a candy-making party, especially around a holiday. Imagine four or five friends in your kitchen—a plate of dark-chocolate pastilles and a good cabernet on hand—working around a table and the stove, sifting, stirring, pouring, smoothing. It's kind of an old-fashioned thing, many hands in the mix, lots of conversations going, and, in the end, much accomplished! Working together is creative, inspiring. For us, it's actually been addictive, to the point where, if we're candy making separately, we sometimes call each other as the caramel or fondant cools, just to check in, touch base. And when we wrap together, we spark each other. One of us will have the perfect lunch box for a batch of Cup-of-Fluffs; the other, a roll of velvet ribbon for parchment-wrapped Toffee Snaps. This kind of inspired sharing is one of the many gifts that will come to you, now that you're crafting your own bars.

Shopping Resources Guide

BAKEWARE AND TOOLS

Madeleine pans: Sur La Table (www.surlatable.com), kitchen stores

Marble slab: Sur La Table (www.surlatable.com), local tile, stone, and kitchen counter retailers, Home Depot (www.homedepot.com)

INGREDIENTS

Barley malt syrup: health food stores, restaurant supply shops such as Restaurant Depot (www.restaurantdepot.com) or those serving bakeries, Surfas (www.culinarydistrict.com)

Chipotle pepper (dried): grocery stores, many online sources such as The Spice House (www.thespicehouse.com)

Dried peas: Trader Joe's or Asian sections of grocery stores. Some dried peas are coated with wasabi paste, which works for our bark recipe on page 78.

Food coloring: kitchen stores, Sur La Table (www.surlatable.com) or India Tree (www.indiatree.com)

Matcha (green-tea powder): online at MatchaSource.com, JapaneseGreenTeaOnline.com, and others

Peppermint oil: Sur La Table (www.surlatable.com), health food stores, or Boyajian (www.boyajianinc.com)

Praline paste: gourmet food stores, bakery supply stores such as Surfas (www.culinarydistrict.com) or Kerekes (www.bakedeco.com), or Nuts.com

Rolled fondant: Kerekes (www.bakedeco.com), Jesters Cake Supply (buyfondant.com), or FondantSource.com

Bibliography

Almond, Steve. *Candyfreak*. New York, NY: Algonquin, 2004.

Benning, Lee Edwards. *Oh, Fudge! A Celebration of America's Favorite Candy*. New York, NY: Henry Holt, 1990.

Beranbaum, Rose Levy. *Rose's Christmas Cookies*. New York, NY: William Morrow, 1998.

Bloom, Carole. *Truffles, Candies, and Confections: Techniques and Recipes for Candymaking*. Berkeley, CA: Ten Speed Press, 2004.

Bowden, Jonny. *The Healthiest Foods on Earth*. Gloucester, MA: Fair Winds Press, 2007.

Boyle, Tish, and Timothy Moriarty. *Grand Finales: A Neoclassic View of Plated Desserts*. Hoboken, NJ: Wiley, 2000.

Brenner, Joel Glenn. *The Emperors of Chocolate: Inside the Secret World of Hershey and Mars*. New York, NY: Crown, 2000.

Broekel, Ray. *The Great American Candy Bar Book*. Boston, MA: Houghton Mifflin, 1982.

Chinn, Carl. *The Cadbury Story*. Birmingham, England: Brewin Books, 1998.

Coe, Sophie D., and Michael D. Coe. *The True History of Chocolate*. London, England: Thames & Hudson, 1996.

Corriher, Shirley O. *BakeWise: The Hows and Whys of Successful Baking*. New York, NY: Scribner, 2008.

Figoni, Paula. *How Baking Works: Exploring the Fundamentals of Baking Science*. Hoboken, NJ: Wiley, 2003.

Friberg, Bo, and Amy Kemp Friberg. *The Professional Pastry Chef: Fundamentals of Baking and Pastry*. New York, NY: Wiley, 2002.

Gisslen, Wayne. *Professional Baking*. New York, NY: Wiley, 2001.

Greweling, Peter P., and The Culinary Institute of America. *Chocolates and Confections: Formula, Theory, and Technique for the Artisan Confectioner*. Hoboken, NJ: Wiley, 2007.

Healy, Bruce. *The French Cookie Book: Classic and Contemporary Recipes for Easy and Elegant Cookies*. New York, NY: William Morrow, 1994.

Hesser, Amanda. *The Essential New York Times Cookbook: Classic Recipes for a New Century*. New York, NY: W.W. Norton, 2010.

Kendrick, Ruth. *Candymaking*. New York, NY: HP Trade Books, 1987.

Kimmerle, Beth. *Candy: The Sweet History*. Portland, OR: Collectors Press, 2007.

Leibovitz, David. *The Great Book of Chocolate*. Berkeley, CA: Ten Speed Press, 2004.

Lopez, Ruth. *Chocolate: The Nature of Indulgence*. New York, NY: Harry N. Abrams, 2002.

McGee, Harold. *On Food and Cooking: The Science and Lore of the Kitchen*. New York, NY: Scribner, 1984.

Mercier, Jacques. *The Temptation of Chocolate*. Brussels, Belgium: Éditions Racine, 2007.

Montagne, Prosper. *La Rousse Gastronomique*. Edited by Jean-Francois Revel. New York, NY: Clarkson Potter, 2001.

Morton, Marcia, and Frederic Morton. *Chocolate: An Illustrated History*. New York, NY: Crown, 1986.

Norris, Susie. *Chocolate Bliss: Sensuous Recipes, Spa Treatments and Other Divine Indulgences*. Berkeley, CA: Ten Speed Press, 2008.

Notter, Ewald. *The Art of the Chocolatier: From Classic Confections to Sensational Showpieces*. New York, NY: Wiley, 2011.

Pollan, Michael. *Food Rules: An Eater's Manual*. New York, NY: Penguin, 2009.

———. *The Omnivore's Dilemma: A Natural History of Four Meals*. New York, NY: Penguin, 2006.

Rain, Patricia. *Vanilla: The Cultural History of the World's Favorite Flavor and Fragrance*. New York, NY: Jeremy P. Tarcher/Penguin, 2004.

Williams, Jimmy, and Susan Heeger. *From Seed to Skillet: A Guide to Growing, Tending, Harvesting, and Cooking Up Fresh, Healthful Food to Share with People You Love*. San Francisco, CA: Chronicle Books, 2010.

Wybauw, Jean-Pierre. *Fine Chocolates, Great Experience*. France: Lannoo, 2006.

Index